Conversation Strategies and Communicative Competence

Christian Jones

Candlin & Mynard ePublishing
Hong Kong

Published by Candlin & Mynard ePublishing Limited
Unit 1002 Unicorn Trade Centre
127-131 Des Voeux Road Central
Hong Kong

ISBN: 9798720382643

Conversation Strategies and Communicative Competence

Copyright 2021 Christian Jones

Candlin & Mynard ePublishing Limited was founded in 2012 and is incorporated as a limited company in Hong Kong (1830010). For further information, please see the website:
http://www.candlinandmynard.com

Cover image: Myoko winter mountains by 雷太 (licensed under CC BY 2.0)

CANDLIN
& MYNARD

Contents

Acknowledgements

This book is dedicated to the late Ron Carter, who helped and inspired so many people in the field of Applied Linguistics and English language teaching. Ron was a fantastic PhD supervisor and mentor to me (and many, many others) and I hope that the work here is a tribute to him in some small way.

It is probably not possible to thank everyone, but I gratefully acknowledge the support, inspiration or friendship of the following people in the past and present: Svenja Adolphs, Marco Antonini, Nick Carter, Ron Carter, Jane Cleary, John Cross, Isabel Donnelly, James Donnithorne, Andy Downer, Graham Ethelston, Nick Gregson, Patrycja Golebiewska, Nicola Halenko, Tania Horak, Douglas Hamano-Bunce, Simon Hobbs, Stuart Hobbs, Nektaria Kourtali, Josie Leonard, Fergus Mackinnon, Hitomi Masuhara, Jeanne McCarten, Michael McCarthy, Tara McIlroy, Marije Michel, Alan Milby, Carmel Milroy, Emma Moreton, Jo Mynard, Clive Newton, David Oakey, Sheena Palmer, Simon Pate, Raymond Pearce, Lesley Randles, Scott Shelton-Strong, Paul Simpson, Karen Smith, Scott Thornbury, Ivor Timmis, Neil Walker, Nicola Walker, Daniel Waller, Andy Williams, Dave Willis.

Thanks to Jeanne McCarten and Michael McCarthy for the foreword and to the participants in each study.

Special thanks to Douglas Hamano-Bunce for initial comments on the manuscript, Katie Hudson for teaching the classes in chapter 4, Jo Mynard for help with data collection in chapter 5 and Ziad Almaki and Zhiming Yang for help with data collection in chapter 4.

Finally, thanks to my family both near and far way, for all of their peace, love and understanding.

The aim of science is not to open the door to everlasting truth, but to set a limit on everlasting error.

Bertolt Brecht

Preface from the Series Editor

Conversation Strategies and Communicative Competence presents four recent studies on the use of conversation strategies and how they affect students' communicative competence and then shows you how to use the activities in your own classes, and possibly do your own research if desired. The author Christian Jones presents and analyses conversation strategies across the spectrum from low-level learners to advanced and native speakers, and very appropriately advises us how to help our students acquire and use valuable strategies in interactive and ecological procedures in our own classrooms. He also includes the research background that any MA or PhD student would need to further study and promote conversation strategies (and I hope that many will).

Jones valuably starts with an overview of what conversation strategies actually are and why we should teach them. He then presents us with a detailed corpus analysis along with teacher evaluations of materials for teaching conversation strategies. He then guides you through two studies with actual students in the classroom in ESL and EFL contexts. Seldom are readers given so many valuable tips, research insights, and pedagogical pathways in conventional research articles; Jones has done a good job of combining good research with valuable pedagogical praxis.

Tim Murphey

The positive pedagogical praxis series

Books in Candlin & Mynard's Positive Pedagogical Praxis Series focus on practical activities, procedures and principles that can create more profound learning in a variety of ways. The books are written in a teacher-friendly style and seek to provide teachers with ways to implement profound ideas into their classrooms. The books could be used for in-service training, professional development workshops and teacher-development.

https://www.candlinandmynard.com/ppp.html

About the Author

Christian Jones is a Senior Lecturer in Applied Linguistics and TESOL at the University of Liverpool, UK. He has been involved in English language teaching for over twenty-five years and has worked in China, Japan, Thailand and the UK. During this time, he has taught general English, business English, exam classes, classes for young learners and undertook materials/course development and teacher training. He holds the Cambridge CTEFLA and DTEFLA qualifications alongside an MA and PhD from the University of Nottingham.

His main research interests are related to spoken language and he has produced work on spoken corpora, lexis and lexico-grammar, classroom applications of corpus data and instructed second language acquisition. Recent publications include: Jones, C., Byrne, S., & Halenko, N. (2018). *Successful spoken English: Findings from learner corpora* (Routledge); *Literature, spoken language and speaking skills in second language learning* (2019) and *Practice in second language learning* (2018) (both as editor, Cambridge University Press).

Foreword

This is a much welcome and timely book that will be of enormous interest to anyone involved in researching and teaching the spoken language in any context. We are delighted to see it published, not just because its rationale, aims and research agenda are dear to our own hearts as language researchers and ELT materials writers, but because it seeks empirical evidence to support the case for successful teaching of conversation strategies, evidence, which in our own case at least, while overwhelmingly positive, has been up to now largely anecdotal.

In the late 1990s as we and our co-author, Helen Sandiford, planned the materials which were subsequently published as *Touchstone* from 2005 and *Viewpoint* from 2012, we were well aware of the problem Christian Jones describes in the preamble, i.e., that students' 'conversations stubbornly refused to develop much beyond question and answer sequences.' To address this, we developed a syllabus strand that we hoped would enable students, even at beginner levels, to engage successfully in the interactive practice that we call 'conversation' as opposed to the vaguer notion of 'speaking.' This meant developing, with the aid of spoken corpora, a new repertoire of language items (e.g., discourse markers, hedges) and techniques (e.g., asking follow-up questions, pre-closing) and a methodology to explicitly deliver them. Any initial scepticism by teachers who had not seen discourse markers such as '*I mean*' in teaching materials or had dismissively referred to them as 'fillers' soon gave way to positive feedback. The hundreds of personal interactions we have had with teachers over the years suggest that teaching conversation strategies really does help learners communicate more effectively, and moreover, that learners and teachers perceive their value. However, this feedback remains at the level of personal communication and by word of mouth.

It is therefore enormously pleasing to see a book which addresses some important research questions in this area including: whether the teaching of conversation strategies is seen as a viable option by teachers working in a range of contexts, to what extent explicit instruction of conversation strategies enhances participants' ability to use them, how learners and ELF speakers use conversation strategies, and whether participants in the studies perceive conversation strategies as useful tools to develop more successful conversations outside of class. These are all valuable questions to seek answers to and the results are instructive.

In Chapter 3 we learn that teachers in different contexts have generally positive attitudes towards a focus on spoken language and teaching conversation strategies. This is important for it is teachers who are the key to successful teaching; they need to believe in the value of the content they are sharing with their learners for it to be effective.

One of the most persuasive aspects of the studies in this book is the prominence of the voice of the learners in the extracts from the learning diaries. So often we approach corpus-informed materials research from a quantitative perspective, number crunching frequencies of words, chunks and patterns or 'before' and 'after' instruction test scores. While these are descriptively and pedagogically illuminating, it is both refreshing and instructive to see in the qualitative data so many comments from actual learners in ESL and EFL contexts. In particular the responses of ESL students in Chapter 4 Study 3, whose language needs we might mistakenly identify as predominantly 'survival' or transactional in nature, show that, on the contrary, they perceive the value of the interpersonal role of conversation strategies. The value these learners attach to this area may also be partly demonstrated by their striking ability to remember not only what they had been taught but also how they had been able to use it outside the classroom. This also shows an impressively high degree of linguistic self-awareness. Similarly, in Chapter 5 Study 4, the Japanese EFL learners report the usefulness of conversation strategies, but interestingly, in connection with reducing the anxiety they felt when called upon to speak; the affective factor in language learning should not be underestimated. Further, these learners considered that the explicit teaching of conversation strategies enabled them to express themselves both better and more naturally, a judgement which surely encapsulates the ultimate aim of all language teaching.

While humbly recognising the limitations of his research studies, Christian Jones draws useful implications to inform the development of materials and inspires a number of avenues for fruitful future research into the teaching of conversation strategies.

We congratulate him on this volume and wish him and anyone connected with conversation strategy teaching huge success. The manifestations of their success will, no doubt, speak for themselves.

Jeanne McCarten
Michael McCarthy

Preamble

When I began teaching (in Japan, in 1993) I came across many learners who wanted to improve their spoken English. They sometimes had the impression that simply by practising the grammar that junior high schools had filled their heads with, often in the dreaded 'conversation' class, their conversation skills would develop naturally. Sadly, they didn't. Looking back, I was aware of this but often lacked the skills to help them effectively. My initial training, while excellent and inspiring in many ways, had suggested that teaching functional exponents, vocabulary or items of grammar such as 'going to' would enable learners to use this in their own conversations, through such methods as contextualisation, concept checking, personalisation and repetition. Of course, I am sure this did help learners to some degree, but I was often left wondering at how their conversations stubbornly refused to develop much beyond question-and-answer sequences. I am not naïve enough to believe that this was solely down to me and am aware of the many factors which may have contributed to this: lack of input, lack of opportunities for interaction in English and motivation being just three of those.

These questions stayed with me and after time, led to reading a seminal article on spoken grammar (McCarthy & Carter, 1995) and then a book (Carter & McCarthy, 1997), both of which gave clear descriptions of spoken language, based on corpus evidence. Eureka! It seems so obvious now. But the revelation that spoken language (especially when used in conversations) has some fundamental differences to written language and that these differences can be described was a breakthrough moment, for me anyway. I understood that we cannot hope to help learners develop good conversation skills if we base teaching on written models, and that we need to understand the interactional and interpersonal nature of conversation. As a previous manager of mine (who shall remain nameless) was fond of saying, this was not rocket science, but it definitely opened a door to me, changing how I thought about language and teaching. Meanwhile, I looked back at some of my old lessons with a creeping despair. All of this sparked an interest which led first to postgraduate and then doctoral study at the University of Nottingham (where Ron Carter and

Mike McCarthy were based) and to a continuing interest in how to help learners to develop spoken language in conversations. This book is the result of that. It represents an investigation into one possible approach aimed at helping learners develop more successful conversations: teaching conversation strategies and the language needed to realise them. I do not claim that this is the only approach or that I have found all the answers – that would be foolish. Research is often about trying to find an answer, being clear on the limits it has and then thinking how we might develop or test that further. I hope that this book achieves at least this.

Introduction

One central aim of Communicative Language Teaching (CLT) is that those employing it seek to help learners develop communicative competence, a concept first developed by Hymes (1972). In order to do this, speaking practice of various forms has often been foregrounded in CLT methodology (used interchangeably with the terms 'communicative methodology/approach/approaches' in this book), in the hope that this will develop communicative competence and therefore the ability to have successful conversations in L2 English. We can, however, question the extent to which syllabuses and common activity types actually do this. We might ask, for example, how many communicative activities actually develop learners' ability to move, in Thornbury's (2005) terms, 'beyond the sentence' or how many are actually based on an analysis of spoken language.

In the last twenty-five years or so, researchers in corpus linguistics (e.g., Carter & McCarthy, 2006, 2017) have done much to describe the most common linguistic and discourse features of conversation, which give us evidence of the forms and functions speakers use when they speak (e.g., Carter & McCarthy 2006, 2017; Jones et al., 2018; Tao, 2003). We now know what native speakers and successful learners say and do when they have conversations, and this is slowly starting to be reflected in teaching materials (e.g., McCarthy et al., 2014). However, as useful as these descriptions are, it is not always clear the extent to which they translate to second or foreign language classrooms, materials and methodology. Burton (2019), for example, argues that the 'cannon' of established pedagogic grammar, as often reflected in textbooks can be impervious to corpus findings and many of us will of course be able to produce examples of stilted and unnatural dialogues in published materials. Regarding methodology and syllabus design, McCarthy and McCarten (2018) suggest that what is termed 'speaking practice' within CLT does not always reflect these findings from spoken corpora. As an example, learners are often given practice of language items at the sentence level, in the hope that they will be able to transfer this into speaking turns and interactive conversation. McCarthy and McCarten (2018) argue against such an approach. They suggest that learners are more likely to develop the ability to have successful conversations if teaching

11

is based on information from corpora and focuses on common conversation strategies (such as showing good listenership) and the language used to realise them. Their work details how such strategies and the language we use for them can be used as an organising principle for conversation syllabuses.

McCarthy and McCarten's (2018) suggestions are persuasive and form one strand of a successful coursebook series (e.g., McCarthy et al., 2014). However, as yet, there is only limited evidence that these ideas have been tested by researchers. The aim of this book is a modest attempt to fill this gap and offer teachers and researchers the start of an evidence base to show the effects of conversation strategies on the communicative competence of both ESL and EFL learners. It is also an attempt to show how different research designs, using quantitative and qualitative data, can be employed to investigate one area in different ways and so provide clearer, more reliable results. Such an approach could of course be applied to other areas which may interest teachers or researchers.

The book begins by introducing the arguments for teaching conversation strategies as a means of developing communicative competence, expanding on some of the ideas mentioned in this brief introduction. This chapter defines key terms and positions this book's aims and arguments. The next four chapters each describe a different study examining the teaching of conversation strategies in a different way: a learner corpus investigation of strategies used by both learners and users of English as a lingua franca; a materials evaluation study based on the responses of teachers in a variety of contexts; an experimental study in an ESL context, comparing the effects of teaching conversation strategies to a control group receiving no instruction; and finally a qualitative diary and interview study in an EFL context. Following this, the concluding chapter discusses the implications of these studies for teachers and researchers.

References

Burton, G. (2019). *The canon of pedagogical grammar for ELT: A mixed methods study of its evolution, development and comparison with evidence on learner output*. [Unpublished doctoral dissertation]. Mary Immaculate College, Limerick, Ireland.

Carter, R., & McCarthy, M. (1997). *Exploring spoken English*. Cambridge University Press.

Carter, R., & McCarthy, M. (2006). *Cambridge grammar of English: A comprehensive guide: Spoken and written English grammar and usage*. Cambridge University Press.

Carter, R., & McCarthy, M. (2017). Spoken grammar: Where are we and where are we going? *Applied Linguistics*, *38*(1), 1–20. https://doi.org/10.1093/applin/amu080

Hymes, D. (1972). On communicative competence. In J. B. Pride & J. Holmes (Eds.), *Sociolinguistics: Selected readings* (pp. 269–29). Penguin.

Jones, C., Byrne, S., & Halenko, N. (2018). *Successful spoken English: Findings from learner corpora*. Routledge.

McCarthy, M., & Carter, R. (1995). Spoken grammar: What is it and how can we teach it? *ELT Journal*, *49*(3), 207–218. https://doi.org/10.1093/elt/49.3.207

McCarthy, M., & McCarten, J. (2018). Now you're talking! Practising conversation in second language learning. In C. Jones (Ed.), *Practice in second language learning* (pp. 7–29). Cambridge University Press.

McCarthy, M., McCarten, J., & Sandiford, H. (2014). *Touchstone second edition, levels 1-4*. Cambridge University Press.

Tao, H. (2003). Turn initiators in spoken English: A corpus-based approach to interaction and grammar. In P. Leistyna & C. F. Meyer (Eds), *Language and computers, corpus analysis: Language structure and language use* (pp. 187–207). Rodopi.

Thornbury, S. (2005). *Beyond the sentence: Introducing discourse analysis*. Macmillan.

CHAPTER 1

What are Conversation Strategies and Why Teach Them?

Introduction

In this chapter, I aim to explain the theoretical basis of this book. In doing so, there is a need to look at several key areas. Firstly, I start by defining conversation strategies and showing how they differ from and are related to more generalised communication strategies. Next, I will define communicative competence (Hymes, 1972) and attempt to show why this theory should still provide an important basis for developing the teaching of conversation within a communicative teaching framework, whichever precise form that takes. Following this, I explore why we might teach conversation strategies as a means of helping to develop communicative competence. Finally, I give one brief example of how this might look in the classroom. As explained in the previous chapter, my aim here is not to argue that this is the only possible approach to developing conversation skills: I am trying to make the argument that this is a plausible way forward.

What are conversation strategies?

The first part of answering this question is to define what is meant by conversation. Although there is no universally agreed definition, it is possible to adapt one from the Cambridge dictionary (2020): "talk between two or more people in which thoughts, feelings and ideas are expressed, questions are asked and answered or news and information is exchanged." We can expand this as follows with two additions in italics: '*unplanned, untimed* talk between two or more people in which thoughts, feelings and ideas are expressed, questions are asked and answered or news and information is exchanged.' We can also employ an adaptation of Thornbury and Slade's (2006, p. 25) definition (italics mine) "Conversation is the kind of speech that happens informally, symmetrically, and *often* for the purposes of establishing and maintaining social ties." These two definitions, which I will adopt in this book, show that conversation does not (normally) have a set time limit, is not something which both parties plan beforehand, is an organised, co-constructed form of discourse and often has an interpersonal goal.

It is also worth making clear that I do not use the term 'conversation strategies' interchangeably with the broader category of communication strategies. These are often defined in a manner which relates to how strategies can solve problems when communicating. Corder (1981, p. 103), for example, suggested that they are "a systematic technique employed by a speaker to express his (or her) meaning when faced with some difficulty." In this sense, they are often linked to strategic competence, a key aspect of communicative competence, which will be explained in full in a subsequent section. In brief, we can define this competence as, at least in part, the ability to repair errors when communicating. Typically, communication strategies will be listed in the research as a taxonomy, such as the one below from Dörnyei (1995, p. 58).

Avoidance or reduction strategies

1. Message abandonment—leaving a message unfinished because of language difficulties.
2. Topic avoidance—avoiding topic areas or concepts which pose language difficulties.

Achievement or compensatory strategies

3. Circumlocution—describing or exemplifying the target object or action (e.g., *the thing you open bottles with* for corkscrew).
4. Approximation—using an alternative term which expresses the meaning of the target lexical item as closely as possible (e.g., *ship* for *sail boat*).
5. Use of all-purpose words—extending a general, empty lexical item to contexts where specific words are lacking (e.g., the overuse of *thing, stuff, make, do*, as well as using words like *thingie, what-do-you-call-it*).
6. Word-coinage—creating a nonexisting L2 word based on a supposed rule (e.g., *vegetarianist* for *vegetarian*).
7. Use of nonlinguistic means—mime, gesture, facial expression, or sound imitation.

8. Literal translation—translating literally a lexical item, an idiom, a compound word or structure from L1 to L2.
9. Foreignizing—using a L1 word by adjusting it to L2 phonologically (i.e., with a L2 pronunciation) and/or morphologically (e.g., adding to it a L2 suffix).
10. Code switching—using a L1 word with L1 pronunciation or a L3 word with L3 pronunciation in L2.
11. Appeal for help—turning to the conversation partner for help either directly (e.g., *What do you call . . . ?*) or indirectly (e.g., rising intonation, pause, eye contact, puzzled expression).

Stalling or time-gaining strategies

12. Use of fillers/hesitation devices—using filling words or gambits to fill pauses and to gain time to think (e.g., *well, now let me see, as a matter of fact*).

A number of studies have shown that instruction of these strategies can help learners to understand and use them (e.g., Dörnyei, 1995; Lam, 2010) and that this can benefit spoken interaction. Taxonomies such as this one from Dörnyei also give teachers and course designers clear ways to organise materials and to design courses for teaching these areas. Some strategies (such as topic avoidance) will of course not need to be taught but will develop via interaction and of course some (such as translation) will commonly feature as a part of many EFL or ESL language classes. There is also no guarantee that awareness of a strategy will enable a learner to use it at the appropriate time. Nevertheless, on balance, research in this area suggests that instruction in these areas can at least speed up the rate at which learners can understand or deploy these strategies and thus improve the spoken interaction which learners undertake.

Conversation strategies differ in some ways from communication strategies. They are less generalised and instead are focused on what specifically happens in conversations. In particular, we can suggest that strategies are used by speakers in areas such as turn taking and turn management, as shown by research in the tradition of conversation analysis (e.g., Liddicoat, 2011; Pstahas, 1995; Sacks et al., 1974). McCarten (2010) and McCarthy and McCarten

(2012, 2018) suggest that the kind of strategies typically used in conversations can be summarised in the following four areas, each broadly relate to how speakers manage turns and the conversation in general. Each area can also be subdivided into sub strategies, an example of which is given below.

Managing the conversation

Ending a conversation: Anyway, better go

Constructing your own turn

Elaborating: I mean, in other words

Taking account of others

Projecting shared understanding: You know, …and that kind of stuff

Showing listenership

Showing you are following: Right, Uh huh

McCarthy and McCarten (2018, p. 14)

Using data from spoken corpora, we can identify the common linguistic realisations of each strategy area. The examples are of some language which analyses of spoken corpora show us are common. Typically this language is a mixture of lexical and lexico-grammatical items. Lexico-grammar has been defined by Halliday and Matthiessen (2004, p. 45) as "patterns which lie somewhere between structures and collocations having some of the properties of both." They give the example of 'take pride/delight + in + -ing,' where we can see the collocates of 'take' are also commonly associated with 'in' and 'ing.' We can see evidence of this in expressions such as 'as I was saying,' which can be used to manage the conversation across turns. A quick search in a corpus such as the Spoken BNC2014 (Love et al., 2017) shows that this form is ten times more frequent than one alternative 'as he was saying.' Of course, not all the strategies listed will have clear linguistic realisations and speakers may use alternative means of managing turns or conversations as a whole. Speakers might, as an example, simply ask questions of the speaker in order to show they are listening and interested or use body language to express this.

It is also clear that there is some crossover with communication strategies. For example, indicating you are thinking about an answer with the use of discourse markers such as 'well' is one obvious way of 'buying time' and of course gestures will commonly be used as a strategy to enhance communication. Overall though, the division which McCarthy and McCarten suggest is useful as it allows us to focus very specifically on what we might teach and research in regard to conversations and how interaction is managed and developed between speakers across and within turns.

Communicative competence

Hymes (1972) is credited with the term 'communicative competence,' a notion which suggests that sociocultural aspects of language use are an integral part of knowing and using any language. According to Hymes, social experiences contribute to both performance (how people use the language) and a language user's internal knowledge (what they know about it) of their first language, even though in a first language, it is highly likely that most knowledge about language will be implicit. This view is summarised in the following quotation:

> We have then to account for the fact that a normal child acquires knowledge of sentences not only as grammatical but also as appropriate. He or she acquires competence as to when to speak, when not, and as to what to talk about with whom, when, where, in what matter. In short, a child becomes able to accomplish a repertoire of speech acts, to take part in speech events, and to evaluate their accomplishment by others... (Hymes, 1972, p. 277)

Subsequent to this work, the theory was developed by Canale and Swain (1980), Canale (1983), Celce-Murcia et al. (1995) and Bachman and Palmer (1996) and orientated towards second language learners. Each theory has subdivided communicative competence into different elements, including aspects such as grammatical competence, sociocultural competence and strategic competence. These theories

18

have been summarised into a four-part model by Jones et al. (2018, pp. 14–15) who suggest we can define communicative competence in relation to spoken language as follows:

1. Linguistic competence – the ability to use language, which includes lexis, grammar, lexico-grammar and phonology effectively;
2. Strategic competence – the ability to repair errors when communicating and also to make appropriate choices which oil the wheels of conversations;
3. Discourse competence – the ability to organise and link language across extended conversational turns;
4. Pragmatic competence – the ability to use language as appropriate for the sociolinguistic context.

The four competences interact and make up communicative competence. To give a simple example applied to conversational language, using the discourse marker '*I mean*' successfully requires a learner to know its form and how it is pronounced (linguistic competence), how to use it to extend their own turn (strategic competence), when to use it in their turn (discourse competence) and whether it is appropriate in the given conversation (pragmatic competence). If a learner only knows one aspect, such as linguistic competence, there is little chance they will be able to fully use or understand an item such as this. They are therefore unlikely to develop what Kramsch (1986) has termed 'interactional competence,' which I use here to mean the ability to take part in successful conversations, at whichever proficiency levels learners are. This is not to say that each of these competences need to be explicitly taught as I will attempt to show in the final part of this chapter but that it will help if we take account of them when planning lessons, courses, activities and materials.

When applied to second language teaching, the view of Hymes and others mentioned previously has provided one theoretical basis for communicative approaches. Put simply, we cannot separate form and use, they are both integral to developing communicative competence. Teaching about any form is flawed unless we show students how to understand or use it in specific social contexts. This is because learners need to know both what is acceptable in terms of form and how language functions in appropriate ways. This has resulted in many procedures which will be familiar to those using communicative approaches in second language teaching, including contextualising target language, checking both form and meaning, information gap activities and role plays (see Brumfit & Johnson, 1979 for an early explanation of a communicative approach). These ideas are still very relevant today and communicative language teaching offers a useful way in which we can consider language, alongside many useful, enjoyable classroom procedures and activities. Despite this, in both materials and teaching courses, linguistic competence is still often given prominence and aspects such as pragmatic competence are neglected (Halenko & Jones, 2017; Halenko et al., 2019). There is also an argument that communicative approaches, as mentioned in the introductory chapter, tend to assume that conversational skills will simply develop via speaking practice (McCarthy & McCarten, 2018), whether used to practise specific language areas or in freer discussions. McCarthy and McCarten (2018) argue that this does not take account of conversational processes or language and that these areas need to be brought to learners' attention as they often go unnoticed.

Why teach conversation strategies?

The first way to answer this question may be to ask ourselves why we want to focus on developing conversation skills with learners. The answer to this is fairly straightforward. Conversations make up a large percentage of common language use (Thornbury & Slade, 2006) and experience tells me (and I imagine many teachers) that the development of speaking skills are often of considerable importance to learners of English. This suggests that they should be a central part of second language teaching and there are a number of reasons why I wish to argue that conversation strategies can provide a useful means by which we develop conversation skills in learners.

Firstly, and probably most simply, the categories which McCarthy and McCarten (2018) offer a means by which we can organise courses or materials in this area. Conversation is, by its nature, messy, as the corpus transcript in Extract 1 shows. It can therefore be difficult to see how we could organise its teaching. Focusing on different strategies provides a means by which we can do this and is one which will make some sense to learners. Extract 1

20

shows the somewhat messy nature of conversation and gives one example of '*I mean*' used to reformulate. It is an extract from a recording of two couples talking about art in a museum, taken from the Spoken British National Corpus 2014 (Love et al., 2017; Spoken BNC2014, 2020).

Extract 1

> S0261: well he he kind of made that clear
> S0262: yeah
> S0261: that it's conservative that
> S0262: and maybe his way of you know flighting to find an audience finding out who is – UNCLEARWORD his stuff I mean there was quite a lot of people there today
> S0261: mm
> S0262: so
> S0261: yeah
> 20262: mm but other than that it's appears like well does he go to school does he go to?
> **I mean** how hoes he what what else does he do to support his kind of message ? –UNCLEARWORD you know like how does he communicate to a big big audience a worldwide audience ? that's not a National Geographic you know co otherwise
> S0261: yeah well I mean the work that he does I mean sure he does assignments for National Geographic but he he's effectively his own man he's effectively freelance I would have thought
> S0262: yeah

Spoken BNC2014, S24A.

The second argument is that, as noted, communicative approaches often come with the assumption that conversation skills will simply develop via speaking practice, however unclearly that is defined. While I have argued that CLT has given us a useful repertoire of activities and a means by which we consider both form and function when we teach, the idea that conversation skills will develop without specific attention seems somewhat hopeful. If we consider the nature of conversation as exemplified in Extract 2, it feels hard to imagine that in the ebb and flow of turn taking, learners will notice common strategies speakers use or how they realise them with particular language forms. Giving them a focus on conversation strategies in the classroom could at least help learners to notice these features, to develop a conscious awareness of how they work and speed up the rate at which they acquire them. Such noticing (the conscious registration of forms in the input) has long been considered a crucial aspect of acquisition (Schmidt, 1990, 1993, 1995, 2001, 2010) as it increases the possibility of converting input to intake. There is some persuasive research evidence (e.g., Schmidt & Frota, 1986; Frota & Yoshioka, 2013) for the benefits of noticing. See also chapter 3 for other studies in this area. Anderson's work on skill acquisition (1993, 1995, 2000, 2004) also provides evidence that shows us that declarative knowledge (in this case conscious knowledge about conversation strategies such as what they are and the language we use to realise them) can become automatised over time so that it becomes procedural knowledge (ability to use them easily and appropriately). This suggests given a focus on this area, and provided with appropriate practice, learners may become better able to use these strategies for themselves, if they choose to do so. I do not wish to imply that this is the only possible way learners can acquire such strategies, but it does give us a rationale for looking at them in the classroom.

The third argument is that strategies allow us to develop all aspects of communicative competence because we are at once considering both form and function. A sequence such as 'as I was saying,' for example, is not very useful unless a learner knows how to say it, how it can be used to manage the conversation, when it is appropriate to use and how it can help to develop a conversation across turns.

In addition, the framework McCarthy and McCarten offer provides a means by which we can use the findings of research in corpus linguistics to help us to develop useful courses and materials. As chapter 2 will discuss in more detail, research into spoken corpora (e.g., Carter & McCarthy, 2006) has shown that the grammar, lexis and lexico-grammar of speech is often different to what we find in written texts. This is particularly true in conversations, which are not prepared, have no set topics and no pre-determined end. We can use the evidence from spoken corpora of different kinds to understand the common linguistic means by which speakers realise particular strategies. Teaching learners this common language is both logical and, we can assume, what the majority of learners would want. Two examples of this are the frequency of formulaic sequences (also termed lexical chunks) such as '*I mean*' and the manner in which many speakers report speech. '*I mean*' is the second most common two-word sequence in the CANCODE corpus of spoken British English (O'Keefe et al., 2007) because it performs an important role in discourse marking, allowing speakers to hold their turn and add more to clarify what they have just said. Speech reporting is often achieved via a lexico-grammatical pattern of 'X was saying/telling me + summary' ('Bobby was telling me about your house') rather than reporting the exact words spoken as in 'She told me she was going to the shops'. These findings, on their own, are of course interesting and useful. Including such items within materials based around conversation strategies can help learners to see how they are used in context and to offer practice in this area.

Lastly, from a research perspective, although corpora provide us with clear data on how people manage and interact in conversations and the language they use, there have only been a limited number of studies which have explored the effects of teaching conversation strategies. Those that do exist have generally found positive effects for this type of material or teaching. Diepenbroek and Derwing (2013) is one example where this was explored via materials evaluation. They examined a range of general English textbooks available in Canada, in order to evaluate how they help with pragmatic development and oral fluency. These books included the *Touchstone* series (McCarthy et al., 2014), which explicitly teaches conversation strategies and is based on the approach explained in this chapter. Their evaluation found that *Touchstone* was the only textbook amongst the twelve surveyed that had a consistent and useful coverage of pragmatic uses of language, largely due to the systematic coverage of conversation strategies. The authors also gave a positive evaluation of the use of corpus data used to inform the language taught in the series.

Wildner-Bassett (1984) and Taylor (2002) both explored the effects of teaching conversational gambits as conversation strategies. Taylor (2002, p. 171) defines gambits as "words or phrases that facilitate the flow of conversation by giving the speaker time to organise his or her thoughts, maintain or relinquish the floor, expound on an argument, or specify the function of a particular utterance." He gives examples such as pause fillers, which in English could include the use of 'well' to buy time. Wildner-Bassett (1984) explored the effects of teaching gambits to learners of German as a second language while Taylor (2002) explored this with learners of Spanish as a second language. Wildner-Basett found a significant increase in quantity and variety of gambits following instruction and Taylor found similar results, when tested via a discussion task. A role-play group showed no significant changes in gambit quantity or variety.

More recently, Talandis and Stout (2015) used an action research model to explore the effect of an intervention on students taking compulsory English classes at a Japanese university from A1– B1 levels. The aim of was to address the difficulty many Japanese learners have in developing simple conversation skills in L2 English via the implementation of a speaking course, featuring new personalised everyday topics, L1 support and the teaching of conversations strategies and the language needed for them, such as listenership and asking for repetition. The results were measured through three cycles of action research over an academic year and via student questionnaires, recorded paired speaking tasks and class notes. The intervention was adjusted after each cycle to better attend to student needs. Results showed a positive perceived benefit of the intervention from the majority of learners, particularly at B1 level, and an increased fluency over time, alongside greater use of taught conversation strategies and less reliance of L1, something which tallied with class notes.

These studies point to the potential of teaching conversation strategies and are encouraging. However, none of the studies mentioned focused soley on examining conversation strategies as described in this chapter. It is for this reason that they are examined in this book. I have made the case in theory and wish to show some evidence that this can work in practice.

How might we teach conversation strategies?

McCarthy and McCarten (2018) suggest that developing conversation skills requires some small changes to typical communicative methodology. Specifically, they mention the need to move on from the notion of speaking practice toward conversation practice. They suggest that a methodology for teaching in this way can be guided by the three principles of Illustration, Interaction and Induction. This slightly edited excerpt from McCarthy and McCarten (2018, p. 12) explains these terms:

Illustration	Conversational extracts are chosen to exemplify a given feature *in context*, supported by corpus evidence, even if the extracts are edited versions of original corpus texts. A single sentence or series of sentences will never truly suffice.
Interaction	This is itself a form of practice. The practice generated is aimed at fostering the habit of interacting with texts, noticing and apprehending key features and using them in the contexts in which they normally occur.
Induction	The practice of awareness skills offers a critical support for this stage, which is a process of incorporating new knowledge into existing knowledge and apprehending underlying principles, whether those principles be formal rules of lexico-grammar or socio-culturally-determined conventions of conversational behaviour.

In the classroom, this might mean undertaking some familiar activities, such as using a conversational extract to illustrate a strategy. The practice of using sample conversations in this way is not new (see Jones, 1977, for example) but the difference suggested is that these are based upon corpus data, even if edited somewhat. I would also argue (e.g., Jones, 2019) that dialogues from literary or TV sources can also be useful, as they often contain many features typical of conversations we find in corpora and can make for motivating materials. Interacting with a model text by asking learners to find or underline or discuss features of texts is also likely to be familiar to many teachers. However, using a text as the basis of encouraging learners themselves to interact is likely to be new, when many practice activities are based on sentence -based examples. Induction activities may involve adapting familiar activities such as personalisation and again, discussion about language, to help learners notice typical strategies as they interact or listen to conversations. Table 1.1 gives an example of this in a sample teaching sequence, with each principle given when used. In this example, only one language item is shown to exemplify the strategy in order to make things as clear as possible.

This sequence is purely illustrative and is not given as a model of how to stage a class of this nature. It simply shows how these principles might work in practice and further examples of this are given in the rest of the book. McCarthy and McCarten (2018) give other samples of teaching material. What it does hopefully show is that such an approach is a means by which we might develop communicative competence in the classroom, as the focus is on language (linguistic competence), strategic competence (managing a conversation), pragmatic competence (appropriacy) and discourse competence (how it refers across turns). These are not explicitly taught but implicit in the way the strategy and language are explored. More specifically, it shows how we could use these principles to develop communicative competence as applied specifically to conversations.

In the rest of this book, I will seek to understand how this competence might develop via the use of conversation strategies, using simple research studies to explore its potential. As mentioned at the start of this chapter and in the introduction, I am not trying to suggest that this is the only way to help L2 speakers develop conversational skills. Learners may (and sometimes do) develop this via extensive interaction in English, for example. Rather, I am trying to investigate it as one plausible way (rather than *the* way) to approach this in the classroom, where many learners will be. In order to investigate this, I have approached this via four different studies: an exploration of conversation strategy use in two spoken corpora, a teacher materials evaluation study, an experimental study in an EFL context and an action research study in an EFL context. These studies follow in the next four chapters.

Table 1.1

Sample Conversation Strategies Sequence Based on Illustration Interaction Induction Principles

Learners read and listen to a conversational extract, adapted or based on a spoken corpus. They are asked to identify who is speaking and what they are speaking about.	**Illustration**
Learners listen again with a transcript and are asked to find examples where speakers refer back to something they said earlier (As I was saying). The speaker is narrating a story about a terrible meal to a friend.	**Interaction**
They are asked to discuss why the speaker does this.	
Learners listen to some similar examples and note how many times each speaker refers back to what they were saying earlier. The class discuss how speakers use this to manage the conversation, often when interrupted as they might be when telling a story. They discuss when we might and might not use this.	
Learners look at transcripts of the conversations and decide what 'As I was saying' links back to in each case.	
Learners listen and practise the typical stress, linking and intonation of this sequence.	
They then use it in mini conversations, similar to the first illustration text.	
Learners plan a similar story. They then tell this to their partner, who asks questions, interrupting them. They then signal their return (if they wish) with 'as I was saying'.	**Induction**
Learners discuss whether they have similar expressions in their first language and if they currently use this in English.	**Induction**

References

Anderson. J. R. (1993). *Rules of the mind*. Lawrence Erlbaum.

Anderson, J. R. (1995). *Learning and memory: An integrated approach*. John Wiley and Sons.

Anderson, J. R. (2000). Implications of the ACT-R learning theory. No magic bullets. In R. Glaser (Ed.), *Advances in instructional Psychology* (pp. 1-27). Erlbaum

Anderson, J. R. (2015). *Cognitive psychology and its implications*. Worth Publishers.

Anderson. J. R., & Fincham. J. M. (1994.) Acquisition of procedural skills from examples. *Journal of Experimental Psychology: Learning, Memory, and Cognition, 20*(6), 1322–1340. https://doi.org/10.1037/0278-7393.20.6.1322

Anderson, J. R., Bothell, D., Byrne, M. D., Douglass, S., Lebiere, C., & Qin, Y. (2004). An integrated theory of the mind. *Psychological Review, 111*(4), 1036–1060. https://doi.org/10.1037/0033-295x.111.4.1036

Bachman, L. F., & Palmer, A. S. (1996). *Language testing in practice*. Oxford University Press.

Bergsleithner, J. M., Frota, S. N., & Yosioka, J. K. (Eds.). (2013). *Noticing and second language acquisition: Studies in honor of Richard Schmidt*. Hawai'i: National Foreign Language Resource Center.

Brumfit, C., & Johnson, K. (Eds.). (1979). *The communicative approach to language teaching*. Oxford University Press.

Cambridge Dictionary (2020). Conversation. In *Dictionary.Cambridge.org dictionary*. Retrieved October 10, 2020, from https://dictionary.cambridge.org/dictionary/english/conversation

Canale, M. (1983). From communicative competence to communicative language pedagogy. In J. C. Richards & R. W. Schmidt (Eds.), *Language and communication* (pp. 2–27). Longman.

Canale, M., & Swain, M. (1980). Theoretical bases of communicative approaches to second language teaching and testing. *Applied Linguistics, 1*(1), 1–47. https://doi.org/10.1093/applin/1.1.1

Carter, R., & McCarthy, M. (2006). *Cambridge grammar of English: A comprehensive guide*. Cambridge University Press.

Celce-Murcia, M., Dörnyei, Z., & Thurrell, S. (1995). Communicative competence: A pedagogically motivated model with content specifications. *Issues in Applied Linguistics, 6*(2), 5–35. http://doi.org/10.2307/3587905

Corder, S. P. (1981). *Error analysis and interlanguage.* Oxford University Press

Diepenbroek, L., & Derwing, T. (2014). To what extent do popular ESL textbooks incorporate oral fluency and pragmatic development. *TESL Canada Journal, 30*(7), 1–20. https://doi.org/10.18806/tesl.v30i7.1149

Dörnyei, Z. (1995). On the teachability of communication strategies. *TESOL Quarterly, 29*(1), 55–85. https://doi.org/10.2307/3587805

Halenko, N., & Jones, C. (2017). Explicit instruction of spoken requests: an examination of pre-departure instruction and the study abroad environment. *System, 68,* 26–37. http://doi.org/10.1016/j.system.2017.06.01

Halenko, N., Jones, C., Davies, L., & Davies, J. (2019). Surveying pragmatic performance during a study abroad stay: A cross-sectional look at the language of spoken requests. *Intercultural Communication Education, 2*(2), 71–87. http://doi.org/10.29140/ice.v2n2.162

Halliday, M. A. K., & Matthiessen, C. (2004). *An introduction to functional grammar* (3rd Ed.). Routledge.

Hymes, D. H. (1972). On communicative competence. In J. B. Pride & J. Holmes (Eds.), *Sociolinguistics* (pp. 269–293). Penguin.

Jones, C. (Ed.). (2019). *Literature, spoken language and speaking skills in second language learning.* Cambridge University Press.

Jones, C., Byrne, S., & Halenko, N. (2018). *Successful spoken English: Findings from learner corpora.* Routledge.

Jones, L. (1997). *Functions of English.* Cambridge University Press.

Kramsch, C. (1986). From language proficiency to interactional competence. *The Modern Language Journal, 70*(4), 366–372. https://doi.org/10.1111/j.1540-4781.1986.tb05291.x

Lam, W. K. (2010). Implementing communication strategy instruction in the ESL oral classroom: What do low-proficiency learners tell us? *TESL Canada Journal, 27*(2), 11–30. https://doi.org/10.18806/tesl.v27i2.1056

Love, R., Dembry, C., Hardie, A., Brezina, V., & McEnery, T. (2017). The spoken BNC2014: Designing and building a spoken corpus of everyday conversations. *International Journal of Corpus Linguistics*, *22*(3), 319–344. https://doi.org/10.1075/ijcl.22.3.02lov

Liddicoat, A. J. (2011). *An introduction to conversation analysis*. Continuum.

McCarten, J. (2010). Corpus-informed course book design. In A. O'Keeffe & M. McCarthy (Eds.), *The Routledge handbook of corpus linguistics* (pp. 413–427). Routledge.

McCarthy, M., & McCarten, J. (2012). Corpora and materials design. In K. Hyland., M. H. Chau, & M. Handford, (Eds.), *Corpus applications in applied linguistic* (pp. 225–241). Continuum.

McCarthy, M., & McCarten, J. (2018). Now you're talking! Practising conversation in second language learning. In C. Jones (Ed.), *Practice in second language learning* (pp. 7–29). Cambridge University Press.

McCarthy, M., McCarten, J., & Sandiford, H. (2014). *Touchstone second edition, levels 1-4*. Cambridge University Press.

O'Keeffe, A., McCarthy, M., & Carter, R. (2007). *From corpus to classroom*. Cambridge University Press.

Psathas, G. (1995): *Conversation analysis*. Sage.

Sacks, H., Schlegoff, E., & Jefferson, G. (1974). A simplest semantics for the organisation of turn taking for conversation. *Language, 50*(4), 696–735. https://doi.org/10.1353/lan.1974.0010

Schmidt, R. W. (1990). The role of consciousness in second language learning. *Applied Linguistics*, *11*(2), 129–158. https://doi.org/10.1093/applin/11.2.129

Schmidt, R. W. (1993). Awareness and second language acquisition. *Annual Review of Applied Linguistics*, *13*, 206–226. https://doi.org/10.1017/s0267190500002476

Schmidt, R. W. (1995). Consciousness and foreign language learning: A tutorial on the role of attention and awareness in learning. In R. W. Schmidt (Ed.), *Attention and awareness in foreign language learning* (pp. 1–63). University of Hawai'i Press.

Schmidt, R. W. (2001). Attention. In P. Robinson (Ed.), *Cognition and second language instruction* (pp. 3–32). Cambridge University Press.

Schmidt, R. W. (2010). Attention, awareness and individual differences in language learning. In W. M. Chan, S. Chi, K. N. Cin, J.

Istanto, M. Nagami, J. W. Sew, T. Suthiwan., & I. Walker (Eds.), *Proceedings of CLaSIC 2010, Singapore, December 2–4* (pp. 721–737). University of Singapore Centre for Language Studies.

Spoken BNC2014. (2020). Retrieved October 10, 2020 from: https://cqpweb.lancs.ac.uk/

Talandis, G., & Stout, M. (2015). Getting EFL students to speak: an action research approach. *ELT Journal, 69*(1), 11–25. https://doi.org/10.1093/elt/ccu037

Taylor, G. (2002). Teaching gambits: The effect of task variation and instruction on the use of conversation strategies by intermediate Spanish students. *Foreign Language Annals, 35*(2), 171–189.
https://doi.org/10.1111/j.1944-9720.2002.tb03153.x

Thornbury, S., & Slade, D. (2006). *Conversation: From description to pedagogy.* Cambridge University Press.

Wildner-Bassett, M. E. (1984). *Improving pragmatic aspects of learners' interlanguage.* John Benjamins.

CHAPTER 2

Study 1. Corpus Analysis

Introduction

In the previous chapter, I explained that the kinds of strategies which McCarthy and McCarten (2018) outline are based on close analysis of corpora, particularly native speaker corpora. This is a welcome application of the information corpora can provide about language. The development of spoken corpora in the last twenty years or so has greatly advanced our understanding of how people speak to each other, the language they use to do so and how this language functions, particularly in conversations. Research has included work on spoken grammar (e.g., McCarthy & Carter, 1995; Carter & McCarthy, 2017); lexis (e.g., Hoey, 2005) and what successful learners and users of English as Lingua Franca (ELF) say (e.g., Jones et al., 2018; Siedlhofer, 2011). A number of open access spoken corpora are now available, allowing teachers and researchers to easily investigate aspects of spoken language (e.g., VOICE 2.0 Online, 2013; Spoken BNC2014). Full references for each corpus are given in the discussion below and links are included in the list of references.

This chapter will focus on analysing the use of conversation strategies by speakers of English as a second language and users of English as a lingua franca. To do so, I will mainly draw upon data from two corpora: The UCLan Speaking Test Corpus (USTC), which contains data from learners who successfully passed speaking tests at CEFR B1–C1 levels (Jones et al., 2018) and VOICE 2.0 Online (VOICE, 2013), which contains conversations from users of English as a lingua franca.

The intention in this chapter is to look at four simple examples of how learners and speakers of ELF employ the strategies of listenership, managing their turns, managing the conversation as a whole and taking account of others and to better understand how this data could inform teaching of these strategies. To do so, I take examples of common linguistic realisations of strategies in USTC (Jones et al., 2018) and employ a mixture of frequency data and close examination of the language items in context, in each corpus. Where applicable, some comparison is made between the two corpora and with data from native speakers in the Spoken BNC2014 (Love et al., 2017). This comparison is intended to simply illustrate usage in each corpus and not to use one corpus as a reference for another.

It is unlikely that all learners or speakers of ELF will have been specifically taught these conversation strategies or the language needed to realise them. This is not important. Successful use is relevant because data from such corpora can be useful in informing what we teach to other, less successful learners and considering how a course or series of lessons on conversation could be built. If we rely solely on native speaker corpora as a model to inform syllabuses and materials, we may produce models of language which some learners cannot or do not need to produce (Jones et al., 2018).

The chapter begins with a review of some previous research in this area and the research questions used in this study. I then explain the methodology used in detail, before finally discussing the results of the analysis and its implications for teaching.

Previous research

As noted in the previous chapter and in the introduction, research in corpus linguistics has provided us with a much better understanding of spoken language in general and conversational language in particular. This is important because intuition is notoriously unreliable; we cannot always remember what we say or how we say something and of course, what an individual says does not always represent how a large number of people speak as they interact.

Work in this area (e.g., Biber et al., 1999; Carter & McCarthy, 2006; McCarthy & Carter, 1995) has shown that that the grammar of speech sometimes differs in significant ways from written language. One example of this is the use of non-restrictive relative clauses in speech. In written form, we would normally expect these to be subordinate to a main clause and unable to stand alone as in the invented example 'My brother, who lives in London, supports West Ham.' In conversations, however, Tao and McCarthy (2001) show that such clauses can stand as single turn, in some cases being linked to a noun phrase which took place several turns earlier in a conversation. This is not a case of speakers using the grammar incorrectly but rather that speakers are using spoken grammar. There are also forms which are accepted as standard in conversational speech but would be ungrammatical in most forms of writing. One example given by Carter and McCarthy (2006) is a header, whereby a noun phrase is spoken first and followed by a pronoun to refer back to it in order to highlight the noun phrase to the listener. An example, based on the one given above could be 'My brother, _he's_ going to London next week'. Of course, there are also many crossovers between the grammar of speech and writing, a point made by Leech (2000) some time ago but overall, the research described has done much to highlight clear areas of difference such as the ones mentioned. At the same time, research into spoken corpora has also shown how much conversational language consists of formulaic sequences, often of two to four words. Wray (2002, p. 9) defines these as "a sequence, continuous or discontinuous, of words or other elements, which is, or appears to be, prefabricated; that is, stored, retrieved whole from memory at the time of use." These sequences (also termed lexical chunks) play important roles in such areas as discourse marking (e.g., _'you know,' 'I mean'_) and, as noted, in realising many of the conversation strategies focused on within this book (e.g., _'as I was saying'_ to manage the conversation). As discussed in the previous chapter, sequences of this type are often lexico-grammatical patterns; we expect certain words in formulaic sequences to go together but also to be found within certain grammatical structures. The sequence 'what happened was', for example, is nearly six times more frequent in the Spoken BNC2014 (Love et al., 2017) than 'what happened is,' obviously due to its function in spoken narration of past events.

As beneficial as this research has been, until relatively recently, much of it has focused on corpora of native speakers. Carter and McCarthy's (2006) comprehensive grammar of spoken and written English, for example, draws upon data (in part) from their CANCODE corpus, consisting of five million words of native speaker speech in various types of speech events. This is not an issue in itself, as such grammars provide vital information on language form and function, but it is also important to understand how other speakers of English use the language. Other researchers have sought to redress this by creating and analysing corpora of non-native speakers, for various purposes. The Louvain International Database of Spoken English Interlanguage (LINDSEI) corpus (see Gilquin et al., 2010) consists of a million words from higher intermediate and advanced learners of English as a foreign language from eleven L1 backgrounds (Bulgarian, Chinese, Dutch, French, German, Greek, Italian, Japanese, Polish, Spanish and Swedish). The data, consisting of three-part interviews with students (set topic, free discussion and picture description) has produced a number of research papers which have investigated features of learner-spoken English. These include research on formulaic sequence use by speakers of English from the UK, India and Germany (Götz & Schilk, 2011) and phrasal verb use by French L1 speakers (Gilquin, 2015). Such research has helped us to understand differences and similarities between native speaker and learner speech.

Seidlhofer et al. (2013) created the VOICE 2.0 Online corpus to investigate spoken English by users of ELF from forty-nine different L1 backgrounds, using English as a common language. The recordings were not scripted and took place in a variety of domains (such as education) and included a variety of speech event types (such as conversation). The corpus contains just over a million words. Researchers have used this data to investigate key lexico-grammatical features of spoken ELF and this has resulted in a number of publications including how word classes may vary in ELF (Osmik-Teasdale, 2014). This research has done much to establish the investigation of ELF as a common variety of spoken English and not something we need to constantly compare to native speaker use.

Jones et al. (2018) created a corpus of successful spoken English (as defined by those learners at a pass level in spoken tests) at CEFR B1–C1 levels. Data was based on paired three-part oral proficiency interviews: a warm up, a paired discussion task and a topic discussion between an examiner and the candidates. The corpus contains close to one hundred thousand words of data and includes a small section of native speakers undertaking the same interviews. There is also a supplementary speech act corpus of thirty thousand words. The data in these corpora was used to investigate how learners at these different levels use language to realise the four main aspects of communicative competence (Hymes, 1972), defined as in this book as a combination of linguistic, strategic, discourse and pragmatic competences. One example finding in this data is that many formulaic sequences remained similar across levels but that the functions expanded as proficiency levels rose so that at C1 level 'I think' and similar chunks could be used to give opinions, hold the floor, to hedge and to seek others' views. This shows us that different levels of proficiency cannot simply be explained by overly simplistic assumptions, including the idea that that learners at higher levels simply know more words or formulaic sequences. It is what learners can do with these sequences which counts. Similar speaking test data has also been gathered by Gablasova et al. (2019) in the 4.2 million word Trinity Lancaster Corpus (TLC). This corpus contains exam data from learners at B1–C2 levels, using the graded examinations in spoken English developed by Trinity College. These exams consist of oral proficiency interviews with candidates undertaking between two and four tasks. It differs from the USTC in size (it is currently the largest corpus of spoken learner interaction) but also in that it contains data from a larger range of levels and L1 backgrounds and also a broader range of marks, at pass, fail and distinction. Research using the corpus has provided valuable information on how learners use English in the tests. Castello and Gesuato (2019), for example, used the corpus to investigate the use of linguistic backchannels (e.g., 'Really?') among B2–C2 level learners from Chinese, Italian and Indian L1 backgrounds. Their findings suggest that Chinese L1 learners of English used backchannels most often, particularly when showing surprise or asking for confirmation. Other studies have so far explored areas such as filled pauses (Götz, 2019) and certainty adverbs (Pérez-Paredes & Díez-Bedmar, 2019). An earlier briefing paper from Gablasova et al. (2014) gives examples of both more and less successful learners in the TLC data and clear pedagogical implications which teachers could use, particularly when preparing learners for such spoken exams. One example finding is that more successful candidates show that they are engaged with the speaker via listenership, using such language as 'uh-huh' and 'yeah.'

These corpora and the research which accompanies them have done much to help us better understand the spoken English of learners and users of ELF. This data is useful simply to understand what different speakers say but also can also help to inform what we teach to learners. We might, for example, use what successful speakers in exams say as a model for learners currently at a lower level of proficiency to (at least) supplement what we know from native speaker corpora.

The aim of this chapter is to build on the research in learner and ELF users corpora in order to investigate how learners and ELF users realise the conversation strategies of listenership, managing your turn, managing the conversation as a whole and taking account of others. There are likely to be many ways in which they do this, including examples such as asking questions of the speaker or reformulating their own turns with discourse markers such as '*I mean*.' However, for the purposes of this chapter, I have focused on one linguistic realisation of each strategy, mainly based on results reported by Jones et al. (2018). These are '*yeah*' (listenership), '*stuff*' (taking account of others), '*what do you think?*' (managing the conversation) and '*and also*' (managing your own turn). This allows me to investigate their use in one learner corpus and one ELF corpus, exploring both frequency and function. This chapter sets out to answer the following research questions:

RQ1. What are the frequencies of '*yeah*,' '*stuff*,' '*what do you think?*' and '*and also*' in the USTC and VOICE 2.0 Online corpora?

RQ2. How do these items function in each corpus?

Following this, conclusions and implications for the teaching of conversation strategies are given.

Methodology

This study uses data from two main corpora: the USTC and VOICE 2.0 Online (2013), as described previously. There are also some examples used from the Spoken BNC2014 (Love et al., 2017) for illustrative purposes. The intention is not to make direct comparisons between the two main corpora as they are quite different in size and in regard to the type of data they contain. Rather, my aim is to show how two different types of L2 users employ the sample conversation strategies of listenership, taking account of others, managing your own turn and managing the conversation as a whole. The approach taken is both quantitative (exploring frequency in both corpora) and qualitative (looking at language in context in order to understand how speakers use the items). Such an approach is beneficial because it can give information on both frequency and function and is one often employed in corpus linguistics (Jones & Waller, 2015).

Corpus information

The USTC corpus consists of 91,173 tokens of learner test data from B1–C1 level and a small sample of native speaker data. All data is taken from speaking tests consisting of oral proficiency interviews. Each test was undertaken by pairs of students with an examiner and consisted of three parts: a warm up, a paired discussion task and a topic discussion between an examiner and the candidates. The same tests were used for the native speaker data. Candidates were marked using standardised global and specific criteria and interrater reliability checked. Only those learners who had achieved a global pass of 3.5 or 4 were included in the corpus (the borderline pass was 2.5 on a scale up to 5). Candidates came from fourteen different L1 backgrounds, including China, Saudi Arabia and Oman and there are almost equal numbers of male and female candidates. See Jones et al. (2018) for a detailed explanation of the corpus. Speaking tests are, of course, not identical to spontaneous conversations in that topics are chosen for participants, they are time bound and an examiner controls the discourse. However, despite these limitations, they do allow us to examine how learners at different levels interact and as the conversations are not rehearsed or scripted, they provide a useful understanding of how they use different conversation strategies.

VOICE 2.0 Online is a corpus containing 1,023,082 tokens of naturally occurring data from ELF users, defined here as those from different L1 backgrounds using English as a means of communication. It is available online and in XML versions. The data is divided into different domains including education and leisure and also different speech event types, including conversations, interviews and seminar discussions. Speakers come from forty-nine different L1 backgrounds, with a near equal amount of male and female speakers. See VOICE (2013) for more details. A corpus of this type has some advantages over test data in that is not controlled by an examiner and is not time bound. Speakers are also not under the pressures of a test and for this reason, we may get a clearer picture of what speakers of this type actually say. Unlike the test data, we cannot distinguish between levels of proficiency, but we can understand what speakers do as they successfully use English as a common means of communication, the most common use of English globally (Seidlhofer, 2005).

Procedure and data analysis

As mentioned, one linguistic item was chosen for each strategy: *'yeah'* (listenership), *'stuff'* (taking account of others), *'what do you think?'* (managing the conversation as a whole) and *'and also'* (managing your own turn). These items were chosen partly based on analysis undertaken by Jones et al. (2018), who explored how successful language learners realised the various aspects of communicative competence. *'Yeah'* is one common way of showing engagement and interest in what others are saying, *'stuff'* is a vague noun, used to refer to things without specifying them exactly, as we presume the listener will know what we mean, *'what do you think?'* is used to share a discussion point with others and bring them into the conversation while *'and also'* is a simple way to add ideas and thus extend your own turn. It was felt that searching for these items was a realistic and limited way to examine how strategies are used. The items were chosen because in Jones et al. (2018) they were found to be of high frequency and in general each item is also easily aligned with its function. There are many other means by which speakers will realise strategies such as listenership (with items such as *'uh huh'* or *'right'*) but as it is impossible to search for functions in a corpus, starting with language and then exploring how it functions is a standard approach.

Each corpus was searched to establish the overall frequency of each item. Examples which did not appear to function as conversation strategies (such as *'stuff'* used as a verb) were excluded from these counts, but all uses of *'yeah'* are included in the initial frequency counts, before looking more closely at how this item functions to show listenership. In the USTC corpus, the native speaker data was not used in the frequency counts and the examiner questions were also excluded. This meant the word count for B1–C1 level was 61,553 words. The frequency of each item per ten thousand words was also calculated using a simple formula given by Evison (2010, p. 126) dividing the total amount of occurrences by the number of tokens in the corpus and multiplying by ten thousand. Normalised frequency such as this allows us to compare how items are distributed more accurately and is generally considered to be a clearer measure of frequency than total counts (Jones & Waller, 2015). In the case of USTC, this frequency data also allowed me to make comparisons across the different learner levels. Following the frequency counts,

39

some simple statistical comparisons were made using log-likelihood calculations. Log-likelihood tells us whether an item is used significantly more (+) or significantly less (-) frequently in one corpus compared with another. The calculation is made using the total frequency counts and takes into account different sizes of corpora (see Rayson & Garside, 2000). The aim here was not to suggest speakers in one corpus should have used the item more or less but to make simple comparisons and observations. Some comparison was also made here with the Spoken BNC2014 (2020), an eleven million word corpus of British native speaker conversations. See Love et al. (2017) for more details.

Following the exploration of frequency, items were examined in context. Concordance lines and the original transcripts were explored to better understand how each item was used to realise the strategy. In the VOICE 2.0 Online data, these were explored only within the speech event type of 'conversation,' which makes up 158,075 words of the total corpus. This allowed me to better understand how the items are used strategically in unplanned discourse without the structure of, for example, a seminar discussion, where the topics may be more controlled.

Results and discussion

RQ1. What are the frequencies of 'yeah,' 'stuff,' 'What do you think?' and 'and also' in the USTC and VOICE 2.0 Online corpora?

Table 2.1 gives the overall frequency and normalised counts for the USTC and the VOICE 2.0 Online data. Normalised frequencies are in brackets. It also contains log-likelihood scores for each item. The + symbol shows greater use in corpus one (USTC) compared to corpus two (VOICE 2.0 Online) while the − symbol shows the reverse. Significance is indicated where this occurs. For reference, the frequencies of each item from the Spoken BNC2014 are also given.

Table 2.1

Overall and Normalised Frequencies and Log-Likelihood Comparisons for 'Yeah,' 'Stuff,' 'What do you Think?' and 'And Also' for the USTC VOICE 2.0 Online and Spoken BNC2014 Corpora

Overall and normalised frequencies	USTC	VOICE 2.0 Online	Log-likelihood comparison (USTC and VOICE 2.0 Online)	Spoken BNC2014
Yeah	1072 (174.15)	15090 (147.49)	(+)26.35*	260,026 (227.64)
Stuff	5 (0.81)	152 (1.48)	(−)2.84	11,277 (9.87)
What do you think?	36 (5.84)	67 (0.65)	(+)81.09*	440 (0.38)
And also	50 (8.12)	307 (3.0)	(+)33.57*	902 (0.78)

*p<.0001

These results show some marked differences in use, the significance of which are confirmed by the log-likelihood scores. It is clear that *'yeah,' 'what do you think?'* and *'and also'* are used significantly more often in the USTC data, when we compare the two corpora. *'Stuff'* is used more in the VOICE 2.0 Online corpus but this difference in frequency of use is not significant.

It is likely that the different levels of use may reflect the different data types included in each corpus. The use of *'what do you think?'* may be more frequent in the USTC because of the nature of the exam data. When the conversation is focused on a discussion task, it is likely that speakers will employ it more than in less controlled situations found in VOICE 2.0 Online, which also includes a wider variety of speech events. The same may be true of *'and also'* – it is commonly employed in both corpora but under exam conditions, speakers may try to extend their turns more often due to exam training and the desire to achieve a better mark. It is well known to learners that in a speaking exam, you can only be judged by what you say so it is wise to try and answer as fully as possible. '*Yeah*' is the most common item by far in both corpora and is likely to reflect a fact discussed in later chapters – showing listenership is highly frequent and something which most learners will have an automatic awareness of from their L1. The significantly higher log-likelihood score in the USTC may again reflect the nature of the data. When learners have to undertake interactive tasks in an exam, this may encourage more listenership in itself and it may also be an exam strategy which learners also adopt. '*Stuff*' is not used significantly more in VOICE 2.0 Online but it is clearly far more frequent. This may reflect a greater awareness of how it can function in spoken discourse among the ELF speakers. It may also be that in an exam situation, learners feel that they should answer accurately and avoid being vague. Given that four of the five examples in USTC come from C1 level learners, it also seems to be an item which lower proficiency learners are less able to use.

When we look at the normalised frequencies of each item in the spoken BNC2014, the figures are higher for '*yeah*' and '*stuff*' but slightly lower for '*what do you think?*' and '*and also.*' The highest frequency item is again '*yeah,*' showing the highly interactive nature of most conversational discourse. '*Yeah*' is clearly one of those small interactional response tokens (McCarthy, 2003) which learners, ELF users and native speakers make a great deal of use of. Such tokens (others would include '*right*' and '*uh huh*') are easy and quick to use and, as we shall see in the next section, can also be made to serve different functions while expressing listenership. The lower frequencies of '*what do you think?*' and '*and also*' may reflect the idea that for native speakers, managing their own turn or inviting others to speak can sometimes be accomplished in less explicit ways, with different lexis and also signalled with intonation. This does not mean that native speakers do not negotiate turn taking or invite others to speak. The following extract from the Spoken BNC2014 gives a good illustration of this in action. In this extract, three speakers are family members, catching up with each other over food and presents. They are discussing how to open something.

Extract 1

S0032: >>yeah the lid like it's vacuum sealed on so you have to ping it off I think I don't really know I did the vacuum sealing bit as then I assumed it would all come off as one bit but I had to sort of
S0094: how weird?
S0032: ping it off with a knife yeah (.) god it's painful
S0094: >>er shall we put that bit back or I dunno?
S0032: dunno I
S0095: that's gone
S0095: it sounded like a tennis ball like packing
S0094: oh yeah
S0021: mm
S0032: thank you very much
S0095: d'you want some --UNCLEARWORD?
S0021: not at the minute thank you

File S23A, Spoken BNC2014

In this short extract, we see that the longer initial turn from S0032, is characterised by its simple additive nature ('you have to ping it off I think I don't really know') followed by 'and then' used to signal a continuation of the turn. After this, it clear that S0094 is not invited to speak explicitly but offers a view about the packaging before the three speakers (S0032, S0094 and S0095) work together to solve the problem, each time commenting on how to unpack the object before S0095 does so. The reason for the lack of explicit signals is partly influenced here by the nature of the discourse. This conversation is clearly an example of what Carter and McCarthy (1997) call 'language in action' speakers talking about something as they do it. The nature of the examination data in USTC does not contain such genres but focuses on interactive discussion topics. Candidates are also unlikely to know each other and so can find it harder to freely contribute in the way the speakers in this extract do. These factors may both contribute to more explicit invitations to speak such as *'what do you think?'*

RQ2. How do these items function in each corpus?

In order to examine the function of each item and show how it is used as a strategy, I will explore each in turn, giving examples from both USTC and VOICE 2.0 Online.

Yeah

In the USTC data, it is noticeable that *'yeah'* occurs more often as levels increase. Jones et al. (2018) note that it is significantly more frequent at B2 and C1 levels than at B1 level. They suggest that this is because as learner levels increase, there is a greater ability to interact and focus on what others are saying alongside formulating your own turn. In terms of listenership, the functions of *'yeah'* also expand with the proficiency levels. At B1, the primary function is to express agreement, while at C1, it is also used to simply show you are following and to extend interaction. Extract 2 shows an example of this in practice at C1 level. Candidates are discussing different tourism options and deciding on what are the most important things to do when deciding where to stay. In this example we can see obvious agreement but also the use of *'yeah'* to extend the ideas of a conversation partner and mutually construct the interaction.

Extract 2

<$9M> Well as for me I think the first thing that we will do is er check the reviews of the hotel. People will send some comments on some websites like there is the hotel dot com.
<$10F> **Yeah** I agree with you in this part but I think maybe the most important one is er the reasonable cost mm because for all the tourists er most of them <$=> are worry about </$=> er care about er +
<$9M> **Yeah** how much <$O13> money </$O13> they will pay for.
<$10F> <$O13> money </$O13> yeah they will pay. I think this this is more expe= er <$O14> important </$O14>
<$9M> <$O14> important </$O14> **yeah.**
<$10F> for others.

<$9M> The hotel rating I think er it wasn't that important than the er the quality of the hotel +

<$10F> **Yeah.**

<$9M> + what do you think?

<$10F> **Yeah.** Yeah of course er this one is important but er erm how about the comfort of the ho= hotel room? Er erm <$=> how </$=> what do you reckon about this one?

Note. + = an overlapped turn, <$10F> etc. = codes for different speakers

USTC

Despite many examples of '*yeah*' used to show listenership, as Jones et al. (2018) maintain, '*yeah*' does of course also have other functions beyond this conversation strategy. Two key functions they identify are linked to learners managing their own turn. '*Yeah*' is used (especially at B1 level in this data) to simply buy time while considering what to say next and also in the formulaic sequence '*so yeah,*' used to signal that a turn has finished.

In the VOICE 2.0 Online corpus, similar listenership functions can be observed. Extract 3 shows '*yeah*' being used to show agreement. In this extract, speakers are discussing types of cheese.

Extract 3

218S4: you <3> you call it different thing </3>

219S2: <3> like some sort of </3> mozzarella? (.)

220S4: yes. =

221S1: = mhm =

222S4: = something like mozzarella <4> but </4> which is like much more consistent (.)

223S1: <4> mhm </4>

224S1: mhm (1)

225S2: **yeah** (.) fat. (2)

Note. (.) = pause of up to half a second, (4), (2) etc. = pause of 4 or 2 seconds
= indicates a turn immediately continued or supported by another speaker

VOICE 2.0 Online EdCon 4 213

In Extract 4 speakers are again discussing food.

Extract 4

383S1: PRETZEL
384S2: **yeah**
385S1: **yeah** it's pretzel. (.)
386S2: but it's with a <spel> b </spel> not a <spel> p </spel> (1)
387S1: e:r we <3> we have it </3> with poppy seed (.)
388S2: <3><LNger> bretzel {pretzel} </LNger></3>
389S1: and with <4> salt </4>
390S2: <4> **yeah** </4> **yeah** (.)
391S1: a:nd with SESAME
392S2: **yeah**
393S1: **yeah** (.)
394S2: **yeah** wit-
395S1: <un> xx </un> **yeah**
396S2: it's like <LNger> bretzel {pretzel} </LNger> not pretzel
397S1: uhu
398S2: with a <spel> b </spel> (.)
399S1: we call <5> it pretzel </5>

Note. (.) = pause of up to half a second, (2) etc. = pause of 4 or 2 seconds
<2> etc. = numbered overlaps
LNger = German Language

VOICE 2.1 Online EdCon 4 385

This example shows how speakers work together to show they are listening, understanding and trying to agree on the explanation being given, while exchanging information about this type of food.

Overall, the data shows that '*yeah*' is highly frequent because it is a multifunctional item, which often serves to show listenership. It can be used to simply show agreement but also to show understanding and extend and develop ideas across turns, helping speakers to manage conversations interactively and mutually. As it is easy to learn and observe others using it, there seems no reason why it should not be taught to learners as one simple way to use the strategy of listenership, as it is clear both learners of English and users of ELF make a great deal of use of the item.

Stuff

The few examples of '*stuff*' in the USTC data show that the learners who did make use of this item used it while taking account of the listener. It was used, as the example in Extract 5 from C1 level shows, when the speaker can assume the listener knows what is being referred to and does not need everything explained in detail. Such explanation would be time consuming and quite dull for the listener. We take account of others when we consider what they might already know and what they might need explained in more specific detail.

Extract 5

<$25F> You can find seven stars hotels and they are really nice they've got lots of things they've got spas they've got swimming pools they've got gym and suites **and stuff** so it's it's really nice <$=> you c= </$=> it attracts lots of people.
<$17M> <$O23> Yeah </$O23>
<$18M> <$O23> Yeah </$O23>
<$25F> Like for me +

USTC

In the VOICE 2.0 Online conversation sub corpus, a number of speakers used '*stuff*' with the same function, to take account of the listener and understand that there is no need to supply all details as we can assume understanding on the part of the listener. There are a total of fifty-three examples of '*stuff*' in this subsection. Extract 6 is one example of this.

Extract 6

105S1:mhm (.)
106S2:they like have the (.) [org2] <2> collec</2>tion
107S1:<2> mhm </2>
108S1:mhm
109S2:website and they have the [org2] education website? (.)
110S3:mhm? =
111S2:= and they brand different types of products
to (.) different erm (.) target groups? (1) for example cos if
erm you have like the COLLECTION website (.) it's the same
as they sell business clothing suits and stuff like that (.) a:nd
for the education website they sell jea:ns t-shi:rts
polo <3> shi:rts </3>
112S1:<3> so </3> you mean
like (.) <pvc> subwebsites </pvc>
113S2:yeah (2)

Note. (.) = pause of up to half a second, (4), (2) etc. = pause of 4 or 2 seconds

<2> etc. = numbered overlaps

<pvc> = indicates following word has phonological variation when pronounced by the speaker
: = a lengthened sound

VOICE 2.1 EdCon 496:111

These examples show that '*stuff*' is often used as part of the
formulaic sequence '*and stuff*' and sometimes within the sequence '*and
stuff like that.*' There are 24 examples of '*and stuff*' in the conversation
section of VOICE 2.0 Online and five examples of '*and stuff like that.*'
The item is also used on its own, normally serving the same function.
The speaker is taking account of the listener because they do not need
to specify in detail the nouns to which they are referring. This is
because they can assume the listener already knows what is meant.
Extract 7 is an example of this.

Extract 7

589S2:then we won't (.)
590S1:o:h i think i go to (.) the laundry (3)
591S3:<soft> (so we also do) </soft>
592S2:good luck
593S1:<@> yeah </@> @@ <6> @@ </6> (1)
594S3:<6><un> xx </un></6>
595S1:put all my stuff in the (.) pf dryer
596S3:mhm

Note. <2> etc. = numbered overlaps
(4), (3) etc. = pause of 3 seconds
@ = laughter

VOICE 2.0 Online LeCon420:781

These uses (particularly from ELF users) show that '*stuff*' alongside '*and stuff*' are commonly used as one means of taking account of the listener. It is interesting that neither the item not the sequences really feature in the USTC data. As mentioned, this may be influenced by the genre. In a test situation, it is understandable that learners may assume that they need to provide only accurate and precise answers. Experience suggests that learners may also be taught to describe things in this way. The usage by ELF users demonstrates how helpful such simple items can be as they allow us to take account of the listener. They are also likely to contribute to fluency as time is not wasted searching for the vocabulary needed to list everything precisely.

What do you think?

Frequency data show that this item is significantly more common in the USTC. This is likely to be due to the nature of this spoken test data, whereby learners are required to undertake paired discussion tasks as part of the tests. Naturally, this will elicit more giving and seeking of opinions than in naturally occurring data. It is also more likely that learners will feel the need to explicitly invite other candidates to give their views as they do not know each other and may feel less able to contribute their own turn. Looking more closely at the USTC data, it is apparent, as Jones et al. (2018) note, that '*what do you think?'* occurs with significantly greater frequency at B2 and C1 levels when compared to B1 levels. This reflects the greater ability of learners at these levels to focus on interaction and the greater need at B1 level for learners to focus on their own turns. They are able to use this as a device to manage the conversation, as extracts 8 (C1) and 9 (B2) show. In the first example, learners are discussing holiday destinations, and in the second home, family and leisure time.

Extract 8

> <$14M> Well in my opinion I prefer the mm location of the hotel and the review of the hotel. Erm er I don't know others but generally every time so I just have my holiday and travel on site I just before that I check the website on the internet and the things I check is the location because I need to make sure that it's really close to er my destination or I I don't want to spend er half hour on road to er drive or walk to the hotel. <$=> That's </$=> I think that's not good. And the other is er you know it's just er when you surfing on the internet of you just can judge the hotel by the by the pictures but <$=> some </$=> most of the time it's not true because picture you can do something work picture and make it beautiful so I prefer the people's review. So that's my opinion what do you think <$=> what do you </$=> **what do you think?**
> <$13M> Yeah personally +
> <$14M> Mm.
> <$13M> + I think the cost is most important for me because you know we are students we don't have eno= enough money to to cost and we have duty to save money because all the money is from our fam= our parents.

Note. + = *an overlapped turn,* <$10F> *etc.* = *codes for different speakers*

USTC (C1)

Extract 9

<$13M> Okay <$E whispers question /$E> Er shall we start?
<$14F> Yeah.
<$13M> Okay er +
<$14F> **What do you think about this?**
<$13M> Er actually er all of you all of us we have a family er and er this family we should spent a lot of time with him because er they know us and er they correct if we do something wrong and er it's okay when you spend a lot of time with family because er er trust you about er yourself and er make you feel comfortable about it and er sometimes it feel worried but er it's quite okay and er now <$=> we are </$=> I try to balance with my friends and with my family and er actually I spend a lot of time with my friends and doing everything and er I enjoy with her and as well I do same things in my family and er sometimes in my family I can go with him anywhere er any place er to see er around er my country and er sometimes my friends er they don't er spend a lot of time to travelling and to go to anywhere because maybe they have a job or as well they have er family and they as well the <$O29> should </$O29>

Note. + = an overlapped turn, <$10F> etc. = codes for different speakers

USTC (B2)

The item functions in a similar way in the VOICE 2.0 Online data. When it does occur, people use it to elicit views in the same way, but it seems that overall, in this corpus at least, there are fewer conversations of a discursive discussion-based nature or, perhaps, speakers feel less need to explicitly bring others into the conversation in this way. Extract 10 shows one example of its use from the conversation sub corpus.

51

441S1: = now wha- **what do you think** about vienna (.) do you like it here? or

442S3: <soft> yeah </soft>

443S2: yeah

444S3: so <1><soft><un> xxxx </un> (.) @@@ </soft></1>

445S2: <1> i well I've been all the day (.) walking </1> around the: (.) the city and it's (.) really great (.) it's a HUGE city (.)

Note. (.) = a pause of up to half a second.
<2> etc. = numbered overlaps
(4), (3) etc. = pause of 3 seconds
@ = laughter

VOICE 2.0 Online PRCon29:441

And also

In the USTC data this item is noticeably more frequent at both B1 and C1 levels, in comparison with B2. There seem to be two different reasons for this. At B1 level, it allows learners to manage their own turn while they develop ideas, particularly in the first part of the exam when answering questions from the examiner. '*And also*' enables candidates to give a longer, more extended answer. At C1 level, it is used across different parts of the exam to extend turns, particularly in the paired discussion sections. Extracts 11 and 12 show examples of this. In the first extract, a B1 candidate is answering examiner (<$0>) questions. In the second, students are discussing good ways to learn a language.

Extract 11

<$0> Okay thank you and <$33F> do you prefer outdoor or indoor activities?

<$33F> Erm I prefer indoor activities because erm if I go outside I have to move a lot and walk a lot <$=> but</$=> **and also** I'm spend a lot of time inside and I <$=> wat= </$=> I usually watching Youtube and also watching films +

Note. + = an overlapped turn, <$10F> etc. = codes for different speakers

USTC – B1

Extract 12

$33M> What do you think about this?

<$32M> Mm I think my opinion is joining a class and talking to native speakers.

<$33M> Yeah I totally agree with you <$E> laughter </$E> because if we join a class we will have a teacher which who is who is a specialist of teaching English **and also** if we talk to native speakers we can we can learn we can learn er natural way to to say the word from native speakers.

<$32M> Yeah I think the same as <$33M> but yeah joining a class is a lot positive thing to us because you're surrounded by other +

Note. + = an overlapped turn, <$10F> etc. = codes for different speakers

USTC – C1

These differences in use are perfectly understandable. At B1 level, we would expect even successful learners to be focused more on answering questions and this is a simple device to help them manage their own turn and to extend answers. At C1, it is still a useful item and allows learners to extend their turn and avoid written additive expressions that they may encounter, such as '*moreover*' or '*in addition.*'

In the VOICE 2.0 Online corpus, '*and also*' is used to extend longer turns but also across shorter conversational turns, to add ideas as speakers think of them and to contribute to the ongoing discourse. Extract 13 shows an example of this.

Extract 13

> 50S1: I've received an email
> 51S2: mhm
> 52S1: er with all the: e:r (.) **and also**: these er (2)
> 53S2: so that I've (ever) i only read it today @@
> 54S1: a:h <@> okay so </@> (1) but you have er already met your buddy? (.)

Note. (.) = a pause of up to half a second.
(4), (3) etc. = pause of 3 seconds
@ = laughter

VOICE 2.0 Online, LECon 405: 52

This use is a method by which speakers can add ideas to a conversation, managing their own turn in tandem with the other speaker(s) in a simple, additive way. Willis (2003) makes clear that by its nature, conversation is additive and as in the Spoken BNC2014 extract above, ideas are often strung together in this way rather than in more elaborate ways which might be employed in writing, via complex sentences, for example.

Conclusion

This chapter aimed to show how language learners and ELF users make use of four sample items to realise conversation strategies. Results show that both learners and ELF users employ these items to create interactive, co-constructed conversations in simple but important ways. The data also show that the frequency of particular items (such as '*what do you think?*') are influenced by the nature of particular genres. Spoken tests featuring discussion tasks are likely to elicit more examples of such language as learners are aware of the need to interact and participate with their partner. As levels progress, the ability to do this is likely to increase, hence its more frequent use. In naturally occurring conversations found in VOICE 2.0 Online and also the Spoken BNC2014, conversations topics are much more varied, and speakers may also not feel the need to explicitly bring others into the conversation. This can be signalled in other ways such as by the use of intonation. Genre also influences lower frequency of use. '*Stuff*' as a means of taking account of the listener is notably less frequent in the USTC data. This could be influenced by the test format and the perception amongst learners that their answers need to be accurate and correct.

Overall, these results suggest that teachers could take account of what learners and ELF users say when designing materials or courses. There is no reason, for example, why transcripts from corpora such as VOICE 2.0 Online cannot be used to illustrate how items such as '*yeah*' are used to show listenership and to develop conversations across turns. Similarly, learner data from higher levels could be used to show lower-level learners how discussions can be developed via the use of items such as '*what do you think?*' Open-access corpus analysis tools such as ANTCONC (Anthony, 2019) can also be used to analyse data which teachers collect for themselves. The VOICE 2.0 Online and USTC data shows how simple ways of managing your own turn such as '*and also*' can be used to extend longer stretches of an individual contribution but also in a simple additive way, to add ideas to an ongoing conversation. Transcripts from corpora such as these or data which teachers develop could be used to illustrate these strategies to learners and teaching sequences and materials could be developed based on such data. If there is resistance from learners or teachers to using learner of ELF data, then of course native speaker corpora mentioned (such as the Spoken BNC2014) are available. However, it is worth bearing in mind that for a number of learners, speakers who are able to undertake conversations at a higher level than they are is often a more realistic and attainable target (Jones et al., 2018).

Clearly, the four items explored here are only some of the ways in which speakers can realise conversation strategies. Further studies could establish in more detail the different ways in which learners and ELF users manage interaction and this would include a more detailed inventory of strategy use. Nevertheless, this chapter has shown that both learners and ELF users do make use of conversation strategies. How we might apply some of these findings to materials and teaching is developed in the next three chapters.

References

Anthony, L. (2019) *AntConc* (Version 3.5.8). Retrieved November 19, 2020 from:
https://www.laurenceanthony.net/software/antconc/

Biber, D., Johansson, S., Leech, G., Conrad, S., & Finegan, E. (1999). *Longman grammar of spoken and written English*. Longman.

Carter, R., & McCarthy, M. (1997). *Exploring spoken English*. Cambridge University Press.

Carter, R., & McCarthy, M. (2006). *Cambridge grammar of English: A comprehensive guide*. Cambridge University Press.

Carter, R., & McCarthy, M. (2017). Spoken grammar: Where are we and where are we going? *Applied Linguistics, 38*(1), 1–20. https://doi.org/10.1093/applin/amu080

Castello, E., & Gesuato, S. (2019). Holding up one's end of the conversation in spoken English. Lexical backchannels in L2 examination discourse. *International Journal of Learner Corpus Research, 5*(2), 231–252. https://doi.org/10.1075/ijlcr.17020.cas

Evison, J. M. (2010). What are the basics of analysing a corpus?. In M. J. McCarthy & A. O'Keeffe (Eds.), *The Routledge handbook of corpus linguistics* (pp. 122–135). Routledge.

Gablasova, D., Brezina, V., & McEnery, T. (2014). *How to communicate successfully in English? An exploration of the Trinity-Lancaster corpus.* http://cass.lancs.ac.uk/wp-content/uploads/2015/02/08-CASS-Trinity.pdf

Gablasova, D., Brezina, V., & McEnery, T. (2019). The Trinity Lancaster corpus: Development, description and application. *International Journal of Learner Corpus Research, 5*(2), 126–158. https://doi.org/10.1075/ijlcr.19001.gab

Götz, S., & Schilk, M. (2011). Formulaic sequences in spoken ENL, ESL and EFL. Focus on British English, Indian English and learner English of advanced German learners. In M. Hundt & J. Mukherjee (Eds.), *Exploring second-language varieties of English and learner Englishes: Bridging a paradigm gap* (pp. 79–100). John Benjamins.

Gilquin, G., De Cock, S., & Granger, S. (2010). *LINDSEI: Louvain International Database of Spoken English Interlanguage*. [CD-ROM]. Presses Universitaires de Louvain.

Gilquin, G. (2015). The use of phrasal verbs by French-speaking EFL learners. A constructional and collostructional corpus-based approach. *Corpus Linguistics and Linguistic Theory, 11*(1), 51–88.

Götz, S. (2019). Filled pauses across proficiency levels, L1s and learning context variables: A multivariate exploration of the Trinity Lancaster Corpus Sample. *International Journal of Learner Corpus Research*, 5(2), 159–180. https://doi.org/10.1075/ijlcr.17018.got

Hoey, M. (2005). *Lexical priming: A new theory of words and language.* Routledge.

Hymes, D. H. (1972). On communicative competence. In J. B. Pride & J. Holmes (Eds.), *Sociolinguistics* (pp. 269–293). Penguin.

Jones, C., Byrne, S., & Halenko, N. (2018). *Successful spoken English: Findings from learner corpora.* Routledge.

Leech, G. (2000). Grammars of spoken English: New outcomes of corpus-oriented research. *Language Learning, 50*(4), 675–724. https://doi.org/10.1111/0023-8333.00143

Love, R., Dembry, C., Hardie, A., Brezina, V., & McEnery, T. (2017). The spoken BNC2014: Designing and building a spoken corpus of everyday conversations. *International Journal of Corpus Linguistics, 22*(3), 319–344. https://doi.org/10.1075/ijcl.22.3.02lov

McCarthy, M. (2003). Talking back: 'Small' interactional response tokens in everyday conversation. *Research on Language in Social Interaction, 36*(1), 33–63. https://doi.org/10.1207/s15327973rlsi3601_3

Pérez-Paredes, P., & Díez-Bedmar M. B. (2019). Certainty adverbs in spoken learner language. The role of tasks and proficiency. *International Journal of Learner Corpus Research, 5*(2), 253–279. https://doi.org/10.1075/ijlcr.17019.per

Seidlhofer, B. (2005). English as a lingua franca. *ELT Journal, 59*(4), 339–341. https://doi.org/10.1093/elt/cci064

Spoken BNC2014 (2020). Retrieved October 10, 2020 from: https://cqpweb.lancs.ac.uk/

Tao, H., & McCarthy, M. (2001). Understanding non-restrictive which-clauses in spoken English, which is not an easy thing. *Language Sciences, 23*, 651–677. https://doi.org/10.1016/s0388-0001(00)00026-7

VOICE 2013. *The Vienna-Oxford international corpus of English* (version 2.0 online). Retrieved October 10, 2020 from: https://voice.acdh.oeaw.ac.at

Willis, D. (2003). *Rules, patterns and words: Grammar and lexis in English language teaching.* Cambridge Language Teaching Library.

Wray, A. (2002). *Formulaic language and the lexicon.* Cambridge University Press.

CHAPTER 3

Study 2. Materials Evaluation

Introduction

Tomlinson (2003, p. 15) defines materials evaluation as a subjective process whereby we "measure the value (or potential value) of a set of learning materials. It involves making judgements about the effect of the materials on the people using them." This is opposed to materials analysis, which focuses on objective facts such as whether a textbook contains listening transcripts or writing activities. It is this definition which is used throughout this chapter. Materials themselves can be defined broadly as "anything which is used by teachers and learners to facilitate the learning of a language" (Tomlinson, 2011, p. 2) but will typically be things such as textbooks, teacher-produced worksheets or videos. In this chapter, the focus is on sample materials which would be used in a classroom to teach learners conversation strategies and the language used to realise them.

Materials evaluation is, of course, a process which most English language teachers (and probably teachers in general) undertake on an informal basis every time they prepare classes. We can probably all identify with both negative and positive evaluations of material we have made before we use them in class. It is also a common topic of discussion in staffrooms after classes but sadly, it is all too rare for such evaluation to be formalised or used in a principled way or to make judgements about materials. This is not the fault of teachers - those running institutions often prefer to impose decisions about materials on them. Research allows us to explore this process in a more systematic manner and therefore examine how teachers in a range of contexts evaluate the same piece(s) of material. In doing so, we can foreground and value teacher judgment and the results give indications about how plausible (or not) teachers in different teaching situations find material, and we can look for common themes within their evaluation. The research is necessarily both qualitative and impressionistic (as it would be virtually impossible for anybody to obtain a representative sample of all English language teachers across the globe) but provided we include a range of teachers as participants, the data can give useful insights into particular approaches used within material.

This chapter is modelled on the approach taken by Timmis (2018), who sought to gain the views of teachers towards a text-based approach to grammar practice, using a qualitative evaluation questionnaire and text-based materials. I take the same approach but have applied this to two samples of material with a focus on conversation strategies. The materials (see appendix 3A) were exemplifications of how we might teach such strategies in the form of two lesson procedures, including activities and texts. They were a means by which teachers could evaluate teaching conversation strategies within their own context. This meant I was more interested in how teachers viewed practice activities or using conversation strategies in general as a means to develop conversation skills rather than such aspects as materials design. One might argue that this could have been achieved via a questionnaire on conversations strategies and teachers' opinions on their use in class, but there were several reasons for avoiding this. Firstly, teachers are often busy and may feel less inclined to answer a more abstract theoretical set of questions. Secondly, in order to find out how plausible (or not) teachers view the teaching of conversations strategies, it makes practical sense to give examples of this in the form of materials. Most of us, if asked to evaluate an idea can do so in more depth if we have an example of how it might work in practice. Lastly, as Tomlinson (2003) (quoting Chomsky) suggests, it is teachers who must accept or reject materials developed based on any form of research.

The chapter begins with a more detailed definition of key terms connected to materials evaluation, before a review of some previous research in this area and the research questions used in this study. I then explain the methodology used in detail, before finally discussing the results of the questionnaire. This section outlines the teacher evaluation in relation to the plausibility of teaching conversation strategies and the questions raised by the teachers' responses.

Previous research

Materials evaluation can be undertaken either pre-use, whilst-use or post-use, or of course a combination of these modes (Tomlinson, 2013). Pre-use evaluation explores the potential of material without requiring teachers to use it. This type of evaluation is undertaken in this study. While other forms of evaluation are obviously valuable, requiring teachers to use the materials could have proved difficult for many and for the purposes of this chapter were not deemed appropriate. Evaluation is often undertaken by teachers but can also be undertaken by learners or a combination of both (see Timmis, 2005 for an example of this). In this study, the views of teachers were sought as I primarily wished to understand how they viewed the teaching of conversation strategies as a means of developing conversation skills. Soliciting the views of learners would also have meant, realistically, organising classes where they used the materials and this was not possible across the range of contexts I sought to cover.

Commonly, it is suggested that materials are evaluated using a checklist with clear criteria (Tomlinson, 2003; McGrath, 2016; Mishan & Timmis, 2015). Ideally, these are developed, trialled and agreed upon groups of evaluators, to remove ambiguity and ensure a consistency of response. Tomlinson (2003) makes a distinction between universal criteria (those which we would apply to materials used in any context) and local criteria (those which apply to our specific context). Examples of universal criteria might be 'To what extent are the materials engaging?' or 'Are the instructions clear for learners?' while local criteria could be a question such as 'Do the materials contain topics likely to interest Japanese high school students?' There is obvious value in developing criteria such as these, for research purposes or for teachers/learners to use if given the opportunity. If developed with care, they can be used to give a clear, principled picture of which materials meet the most criteria set and therefore which are likely to be most effective in any given context. For the purposes of this study, however, a long list of criteria was not given to teachers and instead, a simple qualitative questionnaire was used (see methodology section for more details). There were two main reasons for this. Firstly, given the limited time of most teachers, I felt it was unlikely they would be able to dedicate the time to score materials according to a long list of criteria. Open-ended qualitative questions allowed them to write as much or as a little as they wished. Secondly, I was interested in how teachers would evaluate the plausibility of materials exemplifying the teaching of conversation strategies in relation to their context. Open-ended questions would inevitably allow teachers to express views which are covered by both universal and local criteria, including the clarity of instructions and level of potential engagement by their learners.

There have been a number of publications related to materials development and evaluation in recent years (e.g., McGrath, 2016; Mishan & Timmis, 2015; Tomlinson & Masuhara, 2017). Such publications summarise research and apply it to practice in useful ways, allowing teachers and researchers to have clear guidance on materials development and evaluation. There have also been a number of publications dedicated to studies of materials in various contexts. Tomlinson and Masuhara (2010), for example, edited a volume of studies examining various aspects of materials development in a number of different teaching situations. This includes studies as diverse as the effect of extensive reading programmes for children in the Lebanon and form-focused materials for university students in Japan. The results enable Tomlinson and Masuhara (2010, p. 399) to make broad conclusions such as "authentic texts and tasks stimulate language acquisition if they are relevant and engaging." Other studies have evaluated coursebooks produced for a global market against specific criteria (e.g., Tomlinson et al., 2001; Tomlinson & Masuhara, 2013) and also specific types of materials related to spoken language Timmis (2018), for example, used a questionnaire and asked sixteen teachers across the world (including the UK, Saudi Arabia, Italy and China) to evaluate materials taking a text-based approach to grammar, whereby activities and language were derived from texts chosen primarily for their motivational value and not because they included specific areas of grammar. Teachers had a range of experience, taught various types of classes and included both native and non-native speakers. Results suggested a range of views were held by teachers, which were, on the whole, positive about the approach taken as exemplified by the materials. Overall, their comments indicate that a text-based approach is a viable option and as Timmis (2018, p. 97) states it shows that "text-based language practice is a useful string to have to our bow (amongst many others)." He is quick to acknowledge that he was not setting out to prove that this approach was somehow 'the' answer, even if such as thing could ever really exist. Tomlinson (2019) asked a range of teachers to evaluate materials developed from literature with a focus on enhancing spoken language awareness. The materials exemplified what he terms a text-driven approach, defined as follows:

> A text-driven unit of material is a unit in which a core text is chosen for its potential to achieve affective and meaningful engagement for the target learners. This text (and not a predetermined language point, skill, topic of theme) then drives all the activities in the unit.

(Tomlinson, 2019, p. 39).

Responding to a simple question such as 'would you use this unit with language learners?', teachers from the UK, Vietnam, China and Japan evaluated three short units of text-driven materials. Although there were questions and doubts about the usefulness of some aspects of the units, teachers in general were supportive of the approach and felt it could help to develop pragmatic competence in spoken interaction. Although the sample size was small (eleven teachers), this study, alongside the results of the study by Timmis (2018) indicates that teachers in a range of contexts can view such materials as useful, and different approaches (in this case, text-based and text-driven approaches) as plausible.

There have also been a small number of studies which have evaluated the use of communication and conversations strategies in textbooks (see chapter 2 for a definition of both terms). Faucette (2001), for instance, reviewed the use of communications strategies such as circumlocution in textbooks and found that in general, there was limited coverage or opportunity to practise such strategies, at least in the books she surveyed. More recently, as mentioned in chapter 2, Diepenbroek and Derwing (2013) examined a range of general English textbooks available in Canada, in order to evaluate how they help with pragmatic development and oral fluency. These books included the *Touchstone* series (McCarthy et al., 2014) which explicitly teaches conversation strategies and is based on the corpus research and approach explained by McCarthy and McCarten (2018). Their evaluation found that *Touchstone* was the only textbook which had a clear focus on pragmatic uses of language, largely due to the systematic coverage of conversation strategies. They also gave a positive evaluation of the use of corpus data used to inform the language taught in the series. Such evaluations point to the potential of such materials.

The aim of this study is to build on such research but to place the emphasis on teacher evaluation of materials which exemplify the teaching of conversation strategies. To do so, I have focused on evaluation of two short samples of self-produced materials. Following Timmis (2018), I was seeking to gain an impressionistic understanding of how teachers in a range of contexts responded to such material. In doing so, I sought to answer the following research questions:

RQ1. To what extent is the teaching of conversation strategies to develop speaking skills seen as a viable option by teachers working in a range of contexts?

RQ2. How do teachers respond differently to each sample of material?

Methodology

This study employed a qualitative design. Teachers in a range of contexts volunteered to answer a simple qualitative attitudinal questionnaire and give feedback on two samples of material exemplifying the teaching of conversation strategies. The nature of such surveys is necessarily and deliberately impressionistic (as it is probably impossible to gain a representative sample of all EFL/ESL teachers worldwide) but nevertheless there is value in such impressions, particularly when answering the research questions of the type set in this study. Questionnaires are widely used in second language research (Dörnyei & Taguchi, 2009) and although it may be possible to gain more in-depth responses via interviews, this was not a feasible option in this case, as participants worked full-time in a number of time zones. For this reason, a short questionnaire using open-ended questions was employed as it was felt this was relatively quick and simple for teachers to complete and could, at the same time, elicit their views. As mentioned, there was a decision not to use specific local and general criteria, as it would have been impossible to develop these for every context which participants were working in. Instead, teachers were asked to answer general questions in relation to students they were teaching at the time of the study.

Participants

The sample used here was purposive, in that respondents had to be active EFL or ESL teachers and the aim was to gain a sample from a wide range of contexts, include a range of experience levels and both native and non-native speakers. However, as with many such questionnaires there was a large element of convenience sampling (Timmis, 2018) used alongside this, i.e., I needed to accept responses from those who were available to provide them, having answered email or social media adverts. As a result, it was impossible to gain a perfect balance of, for example, male and female teachers. See Table 3.1 in appendix 3B for details of the participants. Dörnyei and Taguchi, (2009, p. 64), note that such a sample may lead to "self-selection bias," meaning that only those teachers already interested in the type of materials being evaluated would come forward. This could lead to a more positive evaluation than if the sample was more targeted and included, for example, a balance between high school, language school and university EFL/ESL teachers. There is an element of truth to this but as Dörnyei and Taguchi (2009) also note, it is inevitable that all samples contain a large amount of self-selection. We cannot compel participants to complete questionnaires and those who do are always likely to be interested in a project in some way. Provided that the aims of the research project are limited (as they were in this case) and that this potential bias is acknowledged, I would argue that such research has validity.

Procedure

The first stage entailed making the materials. These were constructed by me and consisted of two lesson procedures, with sample exercises and texts, each looking at a different conversation strategy. I choose to use two sample pieces of material as I wished to understand how such materials can be approached in different ways, each within a broadly communicative approach and each employing McCarthy and McCarten's (2018) methodological concepts of Illustration, Interaction and Induction (III). These were explained in chapter 1 but are repeated here for convenience, in the following (slightly edited) excerpt from McCarthy and McCarten (2018, p. 12):

65

Illustration	Conversational extracts are chosen to exemplify a given feature *in context*, supported by corpus evidence, even if the extracts are edited versions of original corpus texts. A single sentence or series of sentences will never truly suffice.
Interaction	This is itself a form of practice. The practice generated is aimed at fostering the habit of interacting with texts, noticing and apprehending key features and using them in the contexts in which they normally occur.
Induction	The practice of awareness skills offers a critical support for this stage, which is a process of incorporating new knowledge into existing knowledge and apprehending underlying principles, whether those principles be formal rules of lexico-grammar or socio-culturally-determined conventions of conversational behaviour.

An example of how this worked in practice can be seen in an extract from Material 1. Note that this is not the entire lesson procedure in order; it has been edited to demonstrate some ways I tried to incorporate the principles. See appendix 3A for the complete set of materials, with all stages included. Further examples of how these principles can be applied to textbook materials can be found in McCarthy and McCarten (2018).

Extract 1 Material 1 (See appendix 3A on page 85 for the full procedure)

You are going to look at a text where two speakers are talking about the weather. It is in a mixed-up order. Put it together so it makes sense. The complete extract is on the next page for you to check. This is taken from a book by Jonathan Coe, a modern British novelist. (Coe, 2007, pp. 161–2).

A. It's my favourite sort.'

C. 'I don't mind summer rain.

F. I remember that she was frowning, and pondering these words, and then she announced:

B. 'Your favourite sort of rain?' said Thea.

E. 'Well, I like the rain before it falls.'

D. In fact I like it.

- How did you decide on the order? Discuss as a group. **Interaction**
- How do you know this is taken from a novel? **Interaction**
- What does the speaker mean when they say 'the rain before it falls'? Do you have a favourite sort of rain? What kind of people do you think these speakers are? Would you like to meet them? **Interaction**
- Find and underline 'in fact'. Why does the speaker use this? What does it mean? Can we use this at the start of a conversation e.g. 'In fact, it's mild today'? **Interaction**
- Practice #2 Ask each other the questions above. Give true answers and use 'well' or 'in fact' when you need to. **Induction**

It is important to emphasise that I treated the concepts of Illustration, Interaction and Induction as *principles* in each set of material and not as lesson steps or stages which needed to be followed in order. For example, the text in Material 1 used to illustrate the strategy was from a novel rather than a corpus but was informed by what we know about conversations from corpus analysis and ways in which speakers manage their own turns. There is also good evidence that conversations from literature often contain many key features of typical conversation and can be motivating as lesson materials (Jones, 2019). The focus on III as three principles meant that Material 1 used an authentic text to illustrate the strategy while Material 2 (see Appendix 3A, page 85) used a scripted dialogue. Material 1 contained steps more similar to presentation and practice and Material 2 used the kind of task-based approach advocated by Willis (1998). I was not interested in contrasting these lesson frameworks, merely in showing different ways in which we might apply III. Several other factors related to these principles informed the creation of the materials. Firstly, there was a deliberate mixture of receptive and productive practice (Jones, 2018). The receptive practice involved the interaction activities, whereby learners were asked questions about the texts such as looking for specific language and discussing its meaning or comparing a form to their L1. The purpose of such activities, as McCarthy and McCarten (2018) note, is to foster habits of noticing within students. As discussed in chapter 1, this belief, after Schmidt (1990, 2010), is that conscious registration of form(s) within the input can help learners to convert form(s) into intake when they encounter them in input and this increases the possibility that they will be able to use such forms, should they choose to. There is good evidence that this process of noticing can contribute to this process and a large field of research has developed to investigate this in various ways, with many finding that increased noticing has a beneficial effect on learners' acquisition (e.g., Indrarathne & Kormos, 2017; Rosa & O'Neill, 1999; Shekary & Tahririan, 2006). See also chapter 1 for other studies in this area.

Questionnaire

Once the materials (see Appendix 3A) were developed, participants were sent a simple, open ended, qualitative questionnaire, adapted from Timmis (2018). Each participant was asked to respond to the following questions about each set of material:

1. Please comment on the materials/procedure as a whole (e.g., texts used, level).
2. Please comment on the language points taught in the activities (e.g., usefulness, level).
3. Please comment on the practice activities themselves (e.g., clarity; usefulness; specific tasks you liked or didn't like).
4. What are your views on taking this kind of approach to conversation skills (in general and in your context)?

These questions were chosen for several reasons. First, they have been used (albeit about text-based materials) by Timmis (2018) and found to elicit a good amount and range of responses. This means they had, effectively, been piloted in another similar study. Second, as the aim was to gain an impressionistic understanding of teachers' views in a range of contexts, quantitative questions such as ranking scales were not appropriate. Finally, I felt the open-ended nature of the questions allowed teachers to say as much or as little as they liked while encouraging open and honest responses.

There is a danger with this type of questionnaire that the responses will be minimal and not provide enough meaningful data. However, as teachers volunteered and therefore had some interest in answering the questions, I felt that this was unlikely. In the event, every participant answered in a reasonable amount of detail, with some contributing quite extensive answers and all providing enough data to be meaningful.

Data analysis

NVivo software (QSR, 2020) was used to sort and code the data. Computer-Assisted Qualitative Data Analysis Software (CAQDAS) software was chosen as it offers a greater level of objectivity than manual coding. CAQDAS software allows us to approach coding in a way which is more systematic and thus more objective than manual coding, creating categories and moving around the data with ease. These codes can then be checked using such tools as word frequency to ensure they accurately represent the views expressed in the data. This frequency data supports the ways in which we might categorise the data, adding a systematic and objective dimension to the analysis. The advantages of CAQDAS are summarised by Kelle (2002, p. 486):

> CAQDAS also helps with the systematic use of the complete evidence available in the data much better than any mechanical system of data organisation. If the data are methodically coded with the help of software, researchers will find evidence and counter-evidence more easily. This clearly reduces the temptation to build far-reaching theoretical assumptions on some quickly and arbitrarily collected quotations from the material.

Following the coding, four main themes emerged, and these are discussed first before the comments are used to answer the research questions. The themes were as follows:

Level

Language focus

Activities

Overall views of the material/approach

Results and discussion

Level

As the target level was not provided or suggested, teachers' comments were based on how they viewed the materials, texts and activities. Level was an area which promoted a very wide range of views, with no absolute consensus, aside from the fact that the material was not suitable for absolute beginners. For Material 1, the majority of comments indicate that it should be used at broadly intermediate level (CEFR B1/B2), with some comments suggesting it could be used at higher levels. Material 2 attracted a broader range of views, with many suggesting it could be used at a number of levels, including elementary and advanced. Most views, however, suggested again CEFR B1 or B2. A selection of teacher comments is given for each material, to give an indication of these views.

Material 1

T1: *I would say that the material is aimed at intermediate/upper-intermediate students, most probably adults taking part in a general English course.*

T5: *I think the lesson could be useful across the B1/B2 broad band (and with teacher adaptation, be useful as a reminder at C1).*

T6: *I'd say it would work well for B1+ or B2 groups.*

T14: *I assume these texts/materials are intended for B1+ students.*

Material 2

T7: *I think this material could be used from A2/B1 onwards.*

T17: *The material, as a whole, is perfect for students around A2+ –B1 level, but I cannot see whether it could be adapted to higher (or lower-level) students.*

T29: *The lesson is also well-written enough that I could easily use it at CEFR B1–C2 with very little change.*

T15: *In my opinion, this exercise can be aimed again at A2, B1 learners but it can still be accommodated to the needs of even B2 learners.*

It is pleasing that the participants' responses suggest that the materials presented are reasonably flexible in terms of level. Conversation skills (as with all language) are something which develop across all learner levels and are not somehow complete by the time learners are intermediate or advanced. For this reason, it may be more fruitful to consider successful strategy use as it applies to each level, so that we talk of more (or less) successful speakers at each level of proficiency. Such a phenomenon is discussed by Jones et al. (2018).

These views also indicate that levels within materials is not an absolute but based on teachers' knowledge of the learners they teach and of proficiency scales such as the CEFR. There is also an important suggestion made in a number of comments that materials used to teach conversation strategies could be used across several levels, with learners interacting with the materials in different ways. A lesson focused on listenership could, for example, introduce the idea at a lower level and then be used for revision purposes at a higher level. This is probably an obvious point for most teachers, but it is not one which is always made clear in published materials, with courses aimed at distinct levels, sometimes giving the impression that learners 'complete' each before they progress. Research in second language acquisition (e.g., Selinker, 1973) has long shown that this is not the case, indicating the need to revise and revisit strategies many times across the levels.

Language focus

There was a generally positive response to the language focus in both materials. This is encouraging, as it suggests that teachers are responsive to the need to focus on spoken language, in a broad range of teaching contexts. The comments also show that dealing with such language in class was generally familiar to the participants and illustrates how applications of spoken corpus linguistics research (e.g., McCarthy & Carter, 1995, 2019; Timmis, 2005) may have had an impact on how a range of teachers view language. A selection of the positive comments are as follows:

Material 1

> T34: *The focus on "in fact" and "well" are very helpful because these expressions are often neglected by EFL students. But in fact they are very important in English conversations.*

> T25: *The target items are certainly useful. They enhance fluency and improve learners' communication. Since my classes are between 60–90 minutes, I would add more similar items such as 'actually.'*

> T24: *I liked the staging for the language-ordering the text gets the students to think of the purpose of 'well/in fact' and then further questions on their meaning.*

> T21: *I like the idea that the material introduces specific strategies engaging in conversations by using "well" and "in fact". These are very useful across year levels in my teaching context.*

Material 2

> T2: *Again, fillers to show good listening, very relevant and important to raise students' awareness.*

> T7: *I think it is useful to train learners to show good listenership from an early stage if they want have success in learning a language fully.*

> T11: *Useful for students who may provide feedback in different ways in their L1 (e.g., Japanese?).*

> T18: *Extremely useful to teach fillers and rejoinders, as it helps learners play for time while they formulate utterances.*

> T23: *There's some great language in this one, especially the non-fluency features and the 'As you said' anaphoric reference. You could do a lot with this and it's quite natural.*

These comments also show that the participants had an awareness of related areas of language which could be taught and the functions of such language. The last comment by T23 about Material 2 also shows that teachers are able to go beyond what is suggested in lesson procedures, if provided with useful, realistic texts which can be used to illustrate spoken language and how it might function strategically.

There were, however, some doubts expressed about the usefulness of the language focused on. These comments were much more noticeable in relation to Material 1. Sometimes this was related to the perceived level of the texts used or the other language in focus within them.

T7: *I thought that starting the lesson with adj+noun collocations for weather was challenging. I don't recall my learners making references to fine rain or heavy snow, so they might find it difficult.*

T27: *The language of the material is a bit high as there are confusing context, but it is useful to develop abstract ideas of emotions and likings at an early age.*

Some also felt the link to conversation strategies was unclear:

T14: *While I believe it is useful for students to practise differentiating "well" and "in fact" I'm not sure how that connects to the idea of managing your turn in conversation. I believe this lexis helps students to clarify certain points or emphasize specific information, which can be helpful in moving a conversation along, but the point of "managing your turn" could have been made more explicit.*

T10: *The language point is useful, but there is little to indicate in the activities that students are receiving any input on turn-taking. Rather, the focus seems to be on talking about the weather.*

Some teachers felt that more language was needed as a central focus:

T25: *I would add more similar items such as 'actually.'*

T17: *The aim of the lesson is to teach the transition words 'well' and 'in fact' as part of making the most of each other's turn during a conversation. Good choice, since students often confuse their use. If possible, I would try to add similar words such as 'actually.'*

T24: *I liked the staging for the language-ordering the text gets the students to think of the purpose of 'Well/in fact' and then further questions on their meaning. I think a wider variety of target language could be used such as 'indeed, actually' etc. for an upper-int class.*

Two teachers also questioned the emphasis on such spoken language. Others questioned the relevance of the topic of weather for their learners.

T31: *In terms of usefulness, this highlights to students a more natural way of expanding on or being more detailed in their answers rather than always using "for example," "like" or "I mean." As much as it is useful, in my opinion, it is also a considerably small component of language in the grand scheme of things.*

T19: *I am wondering whether students will feel whether they had benefited from this lesson as the analysis of the language is focused solely on particular paralinguistic features of English (well/in fact). It is a necessary area for English learners to understand to sound more fluent but greater emphasis may be placed on other areas by the students.*

T4: *I don't know how much the students in my context will find it useful because our small talks are never built around climate. It could be direct and often become personal. So, weather as a conversation topic or even conversation starter is not a familiar task.*

T34: *I might change some words such as "deep snow" since we can't relate to this. We are in a tropical country with wet and dry season only.*

Such criticisms are useful, as they highlight that a materials writer may view something as clear, but this will not always be evident to those using the materials. Whilst the aim of Material 1 was made explicit, it is clear the link between the language and the strategy of managing your own turn was not explicit enough for some. It also shows the importance of being explicit about the how language,

74

strategy and topic relate to each other. In Material 1, the text was chosen first, as one which was potentially interesting. As the topic of this conversation was about the weather, I used this as the topic of the lesson and built on other stages related to that, feeling that talking about the weather was within the reach of most learners, a common conversation topic, and that the dialogue could also usefully illustrate the strategy of managing your turn. However, it is clear that these links needed to be much clearer and to show how language such as 'in fact' can be used to realise this strategy. Some comments also reveal the need to be sensitive to context. While I may consider talking about the weather to be within the reach of most learners, it is clear that a conversation about it will not interest students in certain contexts. This is something that all material writers need to be aware of. If the aim is to help students to have conversations they may wish to have and which are within their reach, local teacher knowledge is vital in informing this. As to whether such language will be important to all teachers and learners, it is obvious that no material can ever be relevant to the needs of all. For this reason, it is important that teachers are given choices about what they teach based on their knowledge of learners, rather than simply being asked to cover material.

Activities

There were a number of fairly detailed comments on the activities and some participants suggested very specific amendments or offered clear criticisms. The general tendency was that participants were positive about the activities and in this sense, it shows that on the whole, they were familiar to teachers and made sense to them. This was shown particularly in relation to Material 2 and there were noticeably more criticisms of Material 1. A sample of the positive comments are as follows:

Material 1

T4: *The practice activities are short and are built on students' previous knowledge. The instructions are clear and students will find it useful if they could distinguish between the use of 'well' and 'in fact.'*

T5: *The procedure as a whole seems to me to be a "well-made lesson," in that it follows a logical structure activating existing knowledge, using a text to exemplify the teaching point and then examining and developing it into practice.*

T6: *I think all of the activities are easy to understand and each have their own benefits.*

T20: *The two practice activities would appear to flow in the typical way: the first asking students to notice and manipulate the target language accurately, the second asking students to perform some expressive task with the target language.*

Material 2

T2: *The fill-in-the-blanks (cloze test) in the practice section is useful as it stimulates a student's ability to work with syntax and grammar – the dialogues are mainly focused on interjections (err..uh..) which allow students to work with informal conversation formats.*

T28: *I really like the practice opportunities. There is a clear framework and structure to follow in practice 1. I think this would give my students confidence and an opportunity to complete the answers to demonstrate their new learning and awareness.*

T31: *The activities presented are extremely clear and give a lot of opportunity for discussions to take place.*

T33: *The practice 2 is good, with another partner, they don't have to listen to the same story again otherwise it feels pretended, they can also practise the conversation skill. And it feels real, because it is possible that their classmates will share their stories about a bad meal.*

The criticisms of activities were related to the choice of texts, design of instructions or activities and ordering. Although some questions were raised about Material 2, most were in relation to Material 1, so it is those which have been included here. Some questioned the use of a literary text as a means of illustrating a conversation strategy:

T8: *I don't think a reading text is the best resource to work with in an oral class – I'd rather use an audio excerpt, perhaps from the audiobook version.*

T7: *I'm wary of learners learning conversation strategies from a novel – a play or an unscripted recording could be better – the descriptive language doesn't benefit task success and could be dropped.*

This is a logical criticism and one which is understandable. The literary dialogue was chosen because (as mentioned previously) it was thought that it would be engaging and also useful to illustrate the conversation strategy. Jones and Cleary (2019) argue that such literary dialogues can be more motivating because they often contain typical conversational language at the same time as representational language (McRae, 1991), that is, language which needs to be interpreted. This is not a new idea and one long argued in second language teaching (e.g., McCarthy & Carter, 1995). There is also evidence that such dialogues can be used to enhance awareness of features of spoken language and can motivate learners (e.g., Jones & Cleary, 2019). However, it is clear that the criticisms made by these participants show the need to choose such extracts with great care, to explain the reason for their inclusion and, if possible, to include a recording of them so learners can fully benefit from their use.

The criticisms of the activity design covered a range of areas. Some were related to the activity in materials one, whereby students were asked to put the conversation in order before reading the correct the version to check their ideas.

T4: *My students might find ordering the jumbled sentences challenging because there are not many contextual clues that they are familiar to do so.*

T13: *The only one I had trouble with was the mixed-up text because I thought it could be a bit misleading. From my point of view, more than one answer could be correct.*

Other criticisms centred on specific activities, such as the following:

T10: *The first three activities have some usefulness as pre-tasks that could build towards a more specific focus but need some linguistic (or I suppose in this case paralinguistic) input (e.g., a grammar point or lexical chunk) related to the conversation strategy (e.g., "Can I say something?") for these activities* to promote uptake of that language. Conducted in sequence as presented, these activities don't seem to build too much of anything.

T12: *For practice 1, sometimes it seems like both answers are OK. (e.g., Well/in fact it's about twenty minutes by bus.) and statements in questions B and D are similar. A different context might be used. Plus all the dialogues start with a Yes/No question, wh- questions can also be used to give the function of using well for time to think.*

T25: *I'm rather sceptical about the usefulness of tasks 6 and 7.*

T28: *It then retains a heavy emphasis on words, what words mean, how they work in different languages, in written and spoken discourse etc. In tasks 10 and 11, the students are asked to insert a couple of words into their speech. In task 12, they are invited to 'use the vocabulary' they came across while speaking. Overall, there is a high risk that following the sequence will not create a meaning-centred learning environment.*

Several participants also questioned the sequencing of activities:

T30: *All the practice activities are good, but I wouldn't necessarily use them all together like this. Activity 1 is a nice warmer to recycle previously taught material and activate schema. Activities 2 and 3 are also useful for this, although the conversation is very abrupt: in a lesson students would be unlikely to close a conversation/topic so quickly.*

T23: *I don't want to get picky, I think there are some fairly good activities in there. I would adapt them differently for use with my students as would any teacher, e.g., make Ex 1 more active/maybe competitive, probably add more drama to the role play, and allow a change of context towards the end (kind of happens in Ex 11) to show the language is transferable to other contexts.*

These criticisms show that overall, the design of Material 1 seemed to have fewer activities which teachers could easily work with and see the logic of. Ordering a conversation, for example, is a familiar activity but it is clear that it can be a frustrating activity if learners might not be able to work out the logical order. This is an issue with literary dialogues, which, by their nature, are not always easy to guess and may follow more creative paths than everyday conversations. This suggests that ordering such dialogues may have questionable value if there are not enough clues in the co-text to help learners with this. Alternatively, if we choose to allow learners to order a dialogue in any way they choose and underline that there is no one correct answer, the aim and intention needs to be transparent. I would argue, after McRae (1991), that there is much value in open-ended tasks when working with literary texts but fully accept that this needs to be made clear to both teachers and learners. This was not the case here. The other criticisms suggest that re-designing these activities so that the aim of each is clearer and contains more language and communicative value would have been helpful in this case.

Overall

As suggested in some of the comments above, there was a generally positive response to the approach taken in these materials (teaching conversation strategies and the language used to realise them in order to develop conversation skills). Having noted this, as with all comments, the overall response was more positive towards Material 2. The comments below illustrate these views:

Material 1

T1: *I often use a similar approach to the one used here, especially when I'm teaching functional language exponents to my students, both on general English and business.*

T3: *The material used is good as it includes an icebreaker, a more contextualized language in use, grammatical points in context, and requires learners to interact together and also reflect on their own language use / cross-linguistic reflection / cross-cultural.*

T5: *The material I have been using has been skipping the step of showing the students these expressions in an authentic context and I prefer this approach (with the context).*

T9: *It's really interesting to see how other teachers are working on incorporating language patterns from the corpora in their lessons. I think a lot of students in my context want to become better speakers and they always appreciate being given tangible ways to improve their spoken fluency. The idea of asking students to model conversations and analyse their own spoken output before they move on to language learning is really interesting as a strategy in speaking lessons.*

T12: *Actually, I am really interested in teaching conversation strategies. I used the course book Touchstone for nearly 4 years, and I really enjoyed teaching its conversation strategies section, and I observed my students improved a lot.*

T14: *I usually use this kind of approach to teaching vocabulary or grammar, but I have never used it to teach conversation skills. By looking at the material and the activities I think this approach would work well in teaching conversation skills.*

Material 2

T1: *In general, this task-based lesson and the task-teach-task setup of the lesson is something I really like and often use in my practice because it puts fluency first.*

T10: *This approach is much more communicative in nature than whatever the approach in Material 1 was trying to be. It is psychologically authentic, repetitious, and genuinely communicative. It also allows for formative feedback.*

T13: *I find the lesson to be practical and enjoyable. I would use it with my B2 teenagers and adults as I think younger students can also relate to the idea of having good or bad dining experiences. I think more explicit work needs to be done in English learning contexts on the interactive nature of having a conversation.*

T25: *I think the structure works well. The model language is relevant. The students have the opportunity to notice key language, think about its meaning, use it in a controlled way and have the chance to practise it. The context is relevant to all students.*

T30: *These materials build well upon each other, with plenty of scaffolding and recycling opportunities. It would also be a fun, interesting lesson with all students having plenty to talk about and stories to tell.*

T34: *Such a meaning-negotiating approach is creative and meaningful. I just think if the students are required to make comparison between their stories and their partners', they need to talk about similar experiences, e.g., unpleasant dining experience at a restaurant.*

The questions raised about Material 1 seemed to centre on the use of interaction activities which were included to foster noticing skills. Examples of these comments are as follows:

T7: *An underlying concern about the whole procedure or methodology, is whether or not I am preparing learners for genuine communication using this process. This depends on lesson aims and course aims, I suppose. Do learners have much chance to share their real thoughts and enjoy participating in a short conversation that has meaning to them?*

T10: *I think spending this much time on noticing takes too much time away from production of the target language at the expense of promoting automaticity. As such, students may leave this activity with a better understanding of what talking about the weather in English can look like, but without any gains in proficiency taking turns.*

T 29: *An attempt at integrating authentic materials (based on BNC and a novel) has been made. Not sure how authentic it would feel for the learner as the metalanguage used (e.g., 'The complete extract is on the next page for you to check') and the level of thinking about the language/literary characters (e.g., 'How is this different to your conversation?' 'What kind of people do you think these speakers are?') seem far more complex than the apparent target language ('well,' 'in fact').*

There were also one or two issues raised with the approach in Material 2. One participant (and this was the only comment like this) questioned the use of a constructed dialogue:

T5: *Food is always a good topic! As I said for the first materials, the procedure is logical and "well-made." Unlike in the first set of materials, there is no source for the exemplar text. Normally, I'd probably not notice as coursebooks usually don't source such conversations from reality. However, having just evaluated the previous lesson, I'm disappointed that this conversation isn't authentic. It is notably scripted, in fact. It would be nicer if it were from reality.*

81

While one felt the whole approach may be difficult to manage in class.

T16: *In my opinion, this is the kind of sequence which sounds well on paper but becomes chaotic in practice both in my teaching context and I would venture saying in general. I have experienced this kind of approaches and usually fail to accomplish its goals.*

The themes above can now be summarised in relation to the research questions set.

RQ1. To what extent is the teaching of conversation strategies to develop speaking skills seen as a viable option by teachers working in a range of contexts?

Undoubtedly, overall, participants did see this that teaching conversation strategies (as exemplified by the materials) is a viable option. This was true for the majority of teachers, who taught a range of classes in a number of EFL and EFL contexts. This is a positive finding as it shows that the kind of approach advocated by McCarthy and McCarten (2018) is viewed as plausible by teachers. This is important because, as Timmis (2018) notes, anything developed based on research has to be found convincing by teachers on the ground. We might advocate the teaching of conversation strategies, but it is teachers who need to feel that such an approach is viable and useful or they will not want to use it.

RQ2. How do teachers respond differently to each sample of material?

There is no doubt that participants responded more positively to Material 2 and overall, found this a more convincing exemplification of a conversation strategies lesson. This is reflected in the word frequency counts of each theme, for each material. For Material 1 the eighth and tenth most frequent words were '*useful*' (37 occurrences) and '*like*' (34 occurrences) while for Material 2, these were the seventh and eighth most frequent words mentioned, with 47 and 45 occurrences respectively. When we look at the word frequency for the overall theme only, *'like'* had 13 occurrences for Material 1 and 20 for Material 2.

There were several reasons for the doubts about Material 1, including concerns about the validity of using a literary dialogue to illustrate the strategy, the value of noticing tasks and the design of the practice activities. Participants did not seem concerned about the use of a scripted dialogue in Material 2 (bar one comment) or more convinced about Material 1 because it used a text from an authentic source. This suggests that for these participants, what was more important was the extent to which the dialogue was representative of the kind of conversation learners need to have (McCarthy & McCarten, 2018). This is important and although probably obvious to many, suggests that any blanket approach which automatically suggests all authentic materials are better than those which are constructed is, at best, naïve. This is not to argue against the use of authentic materials in any way but merely to suggest that scripted dialogues, based on what we know about conversations, and/or adapted from those we find in corpora, can also have a valuable role.

Conclusion

This chapter set out with a simple aim – to check whether teachers in a range of contexts see the teaching of conversation strategies as a viable option to enhance conversation skills. This was based on their pre-use evaluation of two sample materials exemplifying this, developed using the notions of Illustration, Interaction and Induction (McCarthy & McCarten, 2018) as methodological principles, rather than lesson steps or stages. One set of materials was developed based on a dialogue from a novel and attempted to focus on the strategy of managing their own turns and the other used a model dialogue of a task to illustrate the strategy of showing listenership. Teachers were very positive in their evaluation overall, although many more doubts were raised about the first set of material. These doubts centred on concerns about the use of a literary dialogue as a model of conversation and some of the activities included. There was concern expressed by some participants that this material would not help to develop conversation skills as much as Material 2 might.

These results suggest that attempting to develop conversation skills in this way is at least a viable option, particularly if we make use of the kind of procedure exemplified by Material 2. The findings are limited by the nature of such a survey, with a fairly small sample size and the chance that self-selection may have meant the participants were already positively inclined towards materials of this type. Nevertheless, such an impressionistic snapshot of teacher evaluations is, in my view, helpful, as it provides us with an awareness of how teachers view such an approach. If, as I am trying to show in this book, conversation strategies are a useful means by which we can develop conversation skills of learners, then this positive evaluation by teachers suggests this can be more than a theoretical idea.

Appendix 3A

Materials

Material 1

Conversation strategy: Managing your turn

1. Think of words adjectives and nouns connected to the weather, e.g., 'heavy rain,' 'deep snow' etc. Make a list with a partner.
2. Do people commonly talk about the weather in your first language? What do they say? Discuss with a partner.
3. Here is an example of a British chat about the weather (based on a sample from the spoken section of the BYU BNC https://corpus.byu.edu/bnc/). How is this different to your conversation?

> *A It's mild today, isn't it?*
> *B. Yeah*

4. You are going to look at a text where two speakers are talking about the weather. It is in a mixed-up order. Put it together so it makes sense. The complete extract is on the next page for you to check. This is taken from a book by Jonathan Coe, a modern British novelist.

> A. It's my favourite sort.'

> C. 'I don't mind summer rain.

> F. I remember that she was frowning, and pondering these words, and then she announced:

> B. 'Your favourite sort of rain?' said Thea.

> E. 'Well, I like the rain before it falls.'

> D. In fact I like it.

(Complete extract)

'I don't mind summer rain. In fact I like it. It's my favourite sort.'
'Your favourite sort of rain?' said Thea. I remember that she was

frowning, and pondering these words, and then she announced:
'Well, I like the rain before it falls.'

— Jonathan Coe, The Rain Before it falls

Extract from Coe (2007, pp. 161–2).

> 'I don't mind summer rain.
>
> In fact I like it.
>
> It's my favourite sort."
>
> 'Your favourite sort of rain?' said Thea.
>
> I remember that she was frowning, and pondering these words, and then she announced:
>
> 'Well, I like the rain before it falls.'

5. How did you decide on the order? Discuss as a group.
6. How do you know this is taken from a novel?
7. What does the speaker mean when they say 'the rain before it falls'? Do you have a favourite sort of rain? What kind of people do you think these speakers are? Would you like to meet them?
8. Find and underline 'in fact'. Why does the speaker use this? What does it mean? Can we use this at the start of a conversation e.g. 'In fact, it's mild today'?
   Do you use this in English? Do you have an equivalent in your first language?
9. Find and underline 'well'. Why does the speaker use this here? What does it mean? Do you use this in English? Do you have an equivalent in their L1? Both 'in fact' and 'well' are commonly used when we want to organise what we are saying in conversations. We can use 'well' to give an unexpected answer or when we do not wish to say 'yes' or 'no.' 'In fact' can be used to give more information about something we have just said.
10. Practice #1 Choose 'in fact' or 'well' to the replies in these short conversations:
    A.
    Do you like cold weather?
    Well/In fact it's ok I guess but I prefer warmer weather.

B.

Do you enjoy watching films?

Not really, no. **Well/In fact**, the last time I went to the cinema was about 10 years ago.

Really? That's a long time.

C.

Do you live near here?

Well/In fact, quite near I guess. **Well/In fact** it's about twenty minutes by bus.

D.

Do you tend to go out much at weekends?

Not really. How about you?

No, I tend to stay at home. **Well/In fact,** I can't remember the last time I went out.

11. Practice #2

Ask each other the questions above. Give true answers and use 'well' or 'in fact' when you need to.

12. Go back to the conversation. Change the conversation as if you are the speakers. You can use the vocabulary from the start of the class if you wish to, e.g.,

I don't like really heavy rain. In fact, I hate it etc.

Then act this out for the class.

Material 2

Conversation strategy: Showing good listenership

1. Think of a good or bad meal you have had. It could be at home, when eating out or at a friend's house. Prepare to tell your partner about it. Write up to ten key words on a piece of paper to help you. The teacher will help you with vocabulary.
2. Tell your partner about this meal. S/he will also tell you about a good or bad meal s/he has had. Ask each other any questions you like as you listen.
3. Compare and discuss – what was similar about your stories? What was different? Think of three similarities and three differences.
4. Tell the class what these were.
5. Now listen to a similar conversation. What is different about this story compared to yours?
6. Now listen again and look at the transcript as you listen. What language is different compared to the language you used?

Transcript

A. *So, can you remember a good or bad meal you've had?*
B. *Well, it's tricky err…to remember good meals! I can definitely remember a really bad one!*
A. *Uh huh.*
B. *Yeah, it was in London, recently.*
A. *Right.*
B. *Basically, the food was quite expensive and took a long time to arrive. I mean, not forever but at least 45 minutes.*
A. *Really? That's bad. Why was that?*
B. *Well, err, not sure but it was quite busy. But when it finally came it was not very good – the portions were really small and it tasted, you know, salty. We were pretty disappointed.*
A. *Yeah, I can imagine. That's disappointing.*
B. *Anyway, what about you? Have you got an experience like this that you can remember?*
A. *As you said, it's, sort of easy to remember bad ones! I can remember some awful meals, for sure!*

7. Notice how speaker A shows she is listening to speaker B. Underline words and phrases which are used. Are these the same in your first language?

8. List words or phrases here which show:

    We are listening and understanding: *Uh huh,*

    We are listening and want to make a comment about what the other speaker is saying, to show surprise, for example:

9. Which of these phrases do you use when listening? Why do we need to use them?

10. Practice #1

    Add some words or phrases to show speaker B is listening and interested.

A. *So, can you remember a good or bad meal you've had?*
B. *Well, it's tricky. But I can definitely remember one good meal I had recently. We went out for my birthday to a new place in town.*
A. _____
B. *Yeah, it was a bit expensive but well worth it and it was a special occasion.*
A. _____. *What kind of food was it?*
B. *Italian. Mainly pizzas but they also had pasta dishes.*
A. _____. *What did you have?*
B. *A pizza and a salad. Sounds basic but it was really good.*
A. _____. *I really like Italian food. Would you go there again?*
B. *Definitely. I can send you a link to the website if you like.*
A. *Thanks, that would be great!*

11. Practice #2

    Work with a different partner. Tell them about a good or bad meal you have had, as you did at the start of the class. Show you are listening/interested and make comments on what they say.

12. What was similar about your stories? What was different? Think of three similarities and three differences.

Appendix 3B

Table 3.1
Participants

Teacher (T)	Location	Type of teaching	First language	Experience/ qualifications
T1	Spain	CELTA/ general and business English to adults	Hungarian	DELTA/CELTA; 8 years
T2	Turkey	EAP, University	Portuguese	MA ELT; 20 years
T3	Canada	University	Arabic	TESOL certificate, MA Applied Linguistics, Doctorate in Education; 17 years
T4	India	FE College	Malayalam	MA, MPhil, PGDTE, PhD; 10 years
T5	Spain	Primary age students, teenagers and adults, general English, exam groups; one-to-one adults Business English, ESP	English	PGCE, CELTA, DELTA Module 1; 10 years
T6	Online	Online classes, general English to all ages from children to adults, levels: A2-C2	English	CELTA; 3 years
T7	Italy	Corporate English teacher, General English teacher, examiner and Teacher Trainer	English	CELTA, DELTA; 13 years
T8	Germany	University, EAP	English	Trinity College London Cert. TESOL, Dip. TESOL; 13 years
T9	Ireland	Adults general English and exams	Romanian	BA Classical Language, CELTA; 3 years
T10	Japan	University, EFL/EAP/CLIL	English	MA TESOL, 10 years

T 11	UK	University, EAP	English	MSc TESOL, DELTA; 28 years
T12	Turkey	University, EAP	Turkish	Pedagogic Formation Certificate, MA TEFL; 16 years
T13	Spain	Language school, general English, ESP, children and adults	English/ Spanish	BA English/Spanish, CELTA, FELE; 10 years
T14	Greece	Language school, general English	Greek	Undergraduate degree: English language and literature, CELTA; 4 years
T15	North Macedonia	Language school, General English to young learners and teenagers, university	Macedonian	BA in English Language MA in Linguistics; 10 years
T16	Mexico	General English and exams for adults	Spanish	Bachelor's Degree, ICELT with Merit, Delta Module 1; 17 years
T17	UK	University, EAP	Greek	CELTA, DELTA (Modules 1 & 2), TKT Young Learners; 12 years
T 18	Japan	University, EFL and EGAP	English	QTS (Primary), DipTESOL, MA TESOL & App Ling; 17 years
T19	UK	University, EAP	English	MA, Diploma, TYLEC, CELTA; 14 years
T20	Thailand	High school classes and teacher training	English	CELTA, SIT TESOL, Graduate Diploma, MA TESOL; 16 years
T21	Ecuador	Teacher training	Spanish	Bachelor in Pedagogical Sciences with mention in English and French; 14 years

T22	Thailand	EAL/EAP, secondary international school	English	BA English Language and Communication, MSc Reading Language and Cognition, MA Professional Development for Language Education, CELTA, CELTA YL DipTESOL; 10 years
T23	UK	Adult classes, General English and exams	English	CELTA; 8 years
T24	Spain	General, Business English, online classes, all age groups, A2-C1.	Greek	CELTA, DELTA, Special Educational Needs; 6 years
T25	Italy	General English, secondary school	Italian	BA mod foreign lit and lang / PhD Comparative lit/ QTS (UK); 13 years
T26	India	General English, secondary school	English/ Hindhi	B.Ed., PGDME, MA; 25 years
T27	Thailand	EAL, secondary international school Thailand	English	PGCE, CELTA; 11 years
T28	Russia	General English, Business English, ESP, adults and teenagers, language school and high school, adults and teenagers	Russian	ICELT, Delta M1, Delta M2; 16 years
T29	Hong Kong	one-to-one lessons for children 7-18.	English	Cert. TEFL, PGCE ESOL, MA TESOL with Applied Linguistics; 16 years

T30	UK	Language school, General English, Improve your Skills, IELTS, EAP, Academic Study Skills, classes and one to one lessons	English	TrinityCert TESOL, BA TESOL with Modern Languages (Japanese), MA TESOL with Applied Linguistics; 7 years
T31	Brazil	General English and exam classes	Brazilian Portuguese	MA in Linguistics, BA in English Language and Literature, CELTA, TKT; 10 years
T32	China	University, EAP	Chinese	MA TESOL/High School English Teaching Certificate; 3 years
T33	China	University, EFL	Chinese	PhD in EFL teaching, Teacher's Certificate; 20 years
T34	Philippines	High School and college, general English	Iloco/ Ilocano	MA in Education with specialization in ELT. TESOL Certificate, Bachelor of Secondary Education major in English; 7 years

Note

In order to ensure anonymity, I have removed the gender of individual participants but of the thirty-four returned questionnaires, thirteen were male, twenty were female.

93

References

Coe, J. (2007). *The rain before it falls.* Viking.

Diepenbroek, L., & Derwing, T. (2014). To what extent do popular ESL textbooks incorporate oral fluency and pragmatic development. *TESL Canada Journal, 30*(7), 1–20. https://doi.org/10.18806/tesl.v30i7.1149

Dörnyei, Z., & Taguchi, T. (2009). *Questionnaires in second language research: Construction, administration, and processing* (2nd ed.). Routledge.

Faucette, P. (2001). Pedagogical perspective on communication strategies: benefits of training and an analysis of English language teaching materials. *Second Language Studies, 19*(2), 1–40. https://www.hawaii.edu/sls/wp-content/uploads/2014/09/Faucette.pdf

Indrarathne, B., & Kormos, J. (2017). Attentional processing of input in explicit and implicit learning conditions: An eye-tracking study. *Studies in Second Language Acquisition, 39*(3), 401–430. https://doi.org/10.1017/S027226311600019X

Jones, C., & Cleary, J. (2019). Literature, TV drama and spoken language awareness. In C. Jones (Ed.). *Literature, spoken language and speaking skills in second language learning* (pp. 66–95). Cambridge University Press.

Jones, C. (2019) (Ed.). *Literature, spoken language and speaking skills in second language learning.* Cambridge University Press.

Jones, C., Byrne, S., & Halenko, N. (2018). *Successful spoken English: Findings from learner corpora.* Routledge.

Kelle, U. (2002). Computer-assisted qualitative data analysis. In C. Seale, G. Gobo, J. F. Gubrium, & D. Silverman (Eds.), *Qualitative research practice* (pp. 473–489). Sage Publications.

McCarthy, M., & Carter, R. (1995). Spoken grammar: What is it and how can we teach it? *ELT Journal, 49*(3), 207–218. https://doi.org/10.1093/elt/49.3.207

McCarthy, M., & McCarten, J. (2018). Now you're talking! Practising conversation in second language learning. In C. Jones (Ed.), *Practice in second language learning* (pp. 7–29). Cambridge University Press.

McCarthy, M., McCarten, J., & Sandiford, H. (2014). *Touchstone second edition, Levels 1-4.* Cambridge University Press.

McGrath, I. (2016). *Materials evaluation and design for language teaching second edition.* Edinburgh University Press.

Mishan, F., & Timmis, I (2015). *Materials development for TESOL.* Edinburg University Press.

QSR International Pty Ltd. [Computer software]. (2020). *Nvivo* (released in March 2020). Retrieved from: https://www.qsrinternational.com/nvivo-qualitative-data-analysis-software/home

Rosa, E., & O'Neill, M. (1999). Explicitness, intake and the issue of awareness: Another piece to the puzzle. *Studies in Second Language Acquisition, 21*(4), 511–566. https://doi.org/10.1017/s0272263199004015

Selinker, L. (1972). Interlanguage. *IRAL – International Review Of Applied Linguistics In Language Teaching, 10*(1–4), 209–231. https://doi.org/10.1515/iral.1972.10.1-4.209

Timmis, I. (2005). Towards a framework for teaching spoken grammar. *ELT Journal, 59*(2), 117–125. https://doi.org/10.1093/eltj/cci025

Timmis, I. (2018). A text-based approach to grammar practice. In C. Jones (Ed.), *Practice in second language learning* (pp. 79–108). Cambridge University Press.

Tomlinson, B. (Ed.) (2003). *Developing materials for language teaching.* Continuum.

Tomlinson, B. (Ed.) (2011). *Materials development in language teaching.* Cambridge University Press.

Tomlinson, B. (Ed.) (2013). *Applied Linguistics and materials development.* Bloomsbury.

Tomlinson, B. (2019). Literature, text-driven materials and spoken language awareness. In C. Jones (Ed.), *Literature, spoken language and speaking skills in second language learning* (pp. 38–65). Cambridge University Press.

Schmidt, R. W. (1990). The role of consciousness in second language learning. *Applied Linguistics, 11*(2), 129–158. https://doi.org/10.1093/applin/11.2.129

Schmidt, R. W. (2010). Attention, awareness and individual differences in language learning. In W. M. Chan, S. Chi, K. N. Cin, J. Istanto, M. Nagami, J. W. Sew, T. Suthiwan., & I. Walker (Eds.), *Proceedings of CLaSIC 2010, Singapore, December 2-4* (pp.

721–737). University of Singapore Centre for Language Studies.

Shekary, M., & Tahririan, M. H. (2006). Negotiation of meaning and noticing in text-based online chat. *The Modern Language Journal*, *90*(4), 557–573.
http://doi.org/10.1111/j.1540-4781.2006.00504.x

Tomlinson, B., Dat, B., Masuhara, H., & Rubdy, R. (2001). Survey review. EFL courses for adults. *ELT Journal*, *55*(1), 80–101.
https://doi.org/10.1093/elt/55.1.80

Tomlinson, B., & Masuhara, H. (Eds.). (2010). *Research for materials development in language learning*. Bloomsbury Publishing.

Tomlinson, B., & Masuhara, H. (2013). Adult coursebooks. *ELT Journal*, *67*(2), 233–249. https://doi.org/10.1093/elt/cct007

Tomlinson, B., & Masuhara, H. (2017) *The complete guide to the theory and practice of materials development for language learning*. Wiley-Blackwell.

Willis, J. (1998). *A framework for task-based learning*. Longman.

CHAPTER 4

Study 3. Mixed-Methods Study in an ESL Context

Introduction

Chapter 3 focused on a qualitative study, asking teachers to evaluate the potential of teaching conversation strategies, as exemplified in sample materials. As discussed in the introduction, it is also important to evaluate the effects of actual instruction of these strategies. This chapter describes one attempt at doing this. A common method to evaluate the effects of a particular methodology, teaching of certain language or skills is via an experimental study. Such studies have a long tradition in instructed second language acquisition (e.g., Scherer & Wertheimer, 1964) and can be lab or classroom-based, with a focus on real or invented language. Cohen et al. (2007, p. 27) suggest that this type of study normally includes several key features:

1. One or more control groups
2. One or more experimental groups
3. Random allocation to control and experimental groups
4. Pre-test of groups to ensure parity
5. One or more interventions in the experimental groups
6. Isolation, control and manipulation of independent variables
7. Non-contamination between the control and experimental groups

Such studies are important as they enable us to suggest, with some confidence, that the improved test results are largely as a result of instruction. When a number of studies are collected, a meta-analysis can be performed and that can give a more comprehensive body of evidence. In recent years, such studies have become more prevalent and have provided evidence for the benefits of methodologies such as data-driven-learning (Boulton & Cobb, 2017), types of instruction such as explicit teaching (Spada & Tomita, 2010) and the role of interaction and output (Mackey & Goo, 2007) amongst other things. These studies show clearly that instruction can, and often does, have a positive effect on learning. There are of course some caveats we must add in regard to the results of classroom-based studies of this nature with real (as opposed to invented) languages. One limitation is that it is impossible to control variables such as exposure to English outside class. We also obviously cannot generalise the results of one experimental study to all learners in all contexts and even a meta-analysis may not include studies from a broad range of teaching and learning contexts. It is not surprising that many studies are conducted within universities, for example. However, provided groups are equivalent and we control other variables such as level as much as we can, results can be helpful and instructive. They allow us to comment on the effect of instruction in the context of the study, and further studies can then attempt to replicate the result, building the evidence base.

Valuable as experimental studies can be, test results alone only tell us so much. When an experimental study is performed in a classroom setting, we may also wish to understand aspects such as learners' perceptions of instruction and combine test data with qualitative methods such as interviews or diaries. According to Dörnyei (2007, p. 164) one reason for choosing such a mixed-methods design is to "achieve a fuller understanding of a target phenomenon" and a design which also allows for even a small qualitative element can be useful in providing this understanding. Given that the acquisition of language in an instructed context is likely to be at least affected by how a learner responds to what is taught, it is important to understand how a learner perceives the usefulness of any instruction. Mixed-methods design can be balanced between both types of data, or more emphasis can be placed on either data type. Dörnyei (2007) labels the options as:

1. QUANTITATIVE-qualitative

2. QUALITATIVE-quantitative

3. QUANTITATIVE-QUALITATIVE

Obviously, the particular balance should be based on the research questions set, and in all studies, our questions should drive the type of design we choose. This was also the case with the previous studies in chapters 2 and 3. Of course, we also need to take into account what is practically possible in terms of access to participants and the time we have to conduct the research.

This chapter reports on research in an ESL context (the UK). A mixed-methods study (QUANTITATIVE-qualitative) was undertaken, which used a standard experimental design and compared the results of two groups: one receiving explicit instruction in conversation strategies (experimental group) and the language needed to realise them and a control group who received no instruction. Results were measured using a receptive test and a free response spoken test, which gave participants the opportunity to make use of the conversation strategies but did not force them to do so. These were administered at a pre- and post-test stage. In addition, a qualitative measure was used to understand the perceptions of learners about their strategy use in the conversations they were having outside of class. All members of the experimental group kept a simple diary during and after their classes to record conversations they had, the strategies they used and the extent to which they felt the strategies helped.

Results show positive effects for instruction with significant gains made by the experimental group in both test types when compared to the control group at the post-test stage. Diary data indicates that learners in the experimental group could make use of the strategies taught in conversations they had and that they perceived them to be beneficial. However, the test results and diaries also indicate that participants clearly used some strategies more than others and there was evidence that some were avoided.

The chapter begins with a review of some previous research in this area and the research questions used in this study. I then explain the methodology used in detail, before finally discussing the results of the study.

Previous research

As mentioned briefly in chapter one, there have been a number of studies into the effects of instruction of general learning strategies (e.g., Gunning & Oxford, 2014), communication strategies (e.g., Dörnyei, 1995) and strategy use related to specific skills such as listening (e.g., Carrier, 2003) Studies of this nature have taken place in a number of EFL and ESL contexts with a variety of learners and the results have often been positive, showing good effects for strategy instruction when instructed groups are compared to control groups or when measured via qualitative forms of data collection and analysis. Carrier (2003), for example, found significant positive effects for listening strategy instruction with high school students, Chen (2009) found that Taiwanese college students developed their listening strategy use following instruction and Siegel (2013) found that learner perception of listening strategy instruction was positive amongst university students in Japan, when measured by interviews and questionnaires.

A number of these studies have been specifically targeted towards oral interaction. Dörnyei (1995) explored the effect of communication strategy training on instructed and non-instructed groups of Hungarian high school students. Instruction focused on a) topic avoidance and replacement, (b) circumlocution, and (c) using fillers and hesitation devices. The results were measured via speaking tests and learners were also given a questionnaire to assess the perceived usefulness of the instruction. In addition, the speech rate of participants was measured to determine if the instruction had an effect on this aspect of fluency. Results showed a positive and significant benefit for the amount of fillers used when compared to the control groups and the quality (but not amount) of their circumlocution. There was no significant effect on participants' speech rate. Participants valued the instruction and felt it was useful, particularly circumlocution. This demonstrates that instructed strategy training can develop certain aspects of students' spoken language in a positive way and is something learners can also perceive the benefit of. Lam (2010) investigated the effect of instruction on strategies such as asking for clarification and paraphrasing on two groups of lower and higher proficiency secondary school learners in Hong Kong. Effects were measured using stimulated recall interviews. Her findings show that instruction did result in gains in strategy use, particularly among lower proficiency groups. This leads her to suggest that this type of instruction may have more benefit at lower levels as higher-level learners are likely to have already developed strategy use. This finding is logical and gives indications about levels where this type of instruction is best targeted. Logically, up to intermediate levels, learners are likely to have a greater need for particular strategies and the language to realise them. An advanced learner is more likely to have already established a range of strategies for themselves and so are not as likely to be in need of instruction. Gunning and Oxford (2014) employed a mixed-methods study to measure the effects of strategy instruction and how this impacted upon the success of 11-year-old school students in oral interaction tasks in Québec, Canada. Instruction focused on strategies such as asking for help or clarification. Results were measured via pre-and post- oral interaction tests, observations, field notes, interviews and a strategy log, where participants recalled and recorded their own strategy use. Results indicate significantly improved use of strategies from pre-to post-test for the experimental group, a finding largely supported by the qualitative data.

These studies show examples of research in different contexts and how communication strategies can have a positive effect on learners' ability to interact in conversations. They also highlight some of the issues with measuring the effects of such instruction. Dörnyei (1995), for example, discusses the difficulty of testing such strategies as circumlocution, which are optional. This is harder to design into a test than it would be measure learners' use of a form such as past simple as the strategy can more easily be avoided. This is an issue I will return to when describing the methodology used in this study.

Research specifically focused on conversation strategies as described by McCarthy and McCarten (2018) is noticeably thinner on the ground than research into the broader categories described above. As mentioned in chapters 2 and 3, they suggest that a syllabus can be built around four main areas of conversation strategies and the language used to realise them can be best understood by analysing corpus data. They give examples of the strategies as follows:

Strategy: Showing listenership. Sample language: *Uh huh, Really? That's interesting, Wow!*

Strategy: Managing the conversation. Sample language: *As I was saying, Anyway.*

Strategy: Managing your own turn. Sample language: *I mean, What I mean is.*

Strategy: Taking account of others. Sample language: I like jazz *and that kind of thing.*

In chapters 2 and 3, it was mentioned that there have been a small number of studies which have examined the effects of conversation strategy instruction and evaluated their use in materials (Diepenbroek & Derwing, 2014; Talandis & Stout, 2015; Taylor, 2002; Wildner-Bassett, 1984). This research has, in general, found positive effects for instruction in this area and given a positive evaluation of teaching material featuring conversation strategies.

Other studies have explored various aspects of spoken language and ways in which this can be learnt via instruction. While these have not focused directly on the kind of strategy use explained by McCarthy and McCarten (2018), they have involved dealing with similar, corpus-informed spoken language. As such, they give useful results which can at least inform the current study. Timmis (2005) developed materials based on videos and employed a framework of cultural access tasks, global understanding tasks, noticing tasks and language discussion task, each looking at various aspects of spoken language which corpora show are frequent. This included features such as ellipsis, where words are missed out depending on context and situation. For instance, when ordering a coffee or similar it is not normally necessary to produce an over-elaborate request such as 'I wonder if I could have a coffee please?' because the situation demands speed and so '(Can I have) Two coffees please' (or similar) will often suffice. Timmis piloted these materials with six teachers based in the UK and Austria and approximately sixty learners and then surveyed them for their responses. Data from learners and teachers show that reactions to the materials were generally very positive with comments clearly indicating that they had helped learners to notice features such as ellipsis, which they may previously have missed. Although he did not categorise the use of ellipsis as a conversation strategy, its use (or non-use) is part of how we take account of others.

Jones and Carter (2014) investigated the teaching of spoken discourse markers such as '*right*' and '*you know,*' many of which fulfil the kind of conversation strategies mentioned. '*Right,*' for example, can be used to show listenership. In a comparison of Present Practice Produce (PPP) and Illustration Interaction Induction (III) methodologies, they used test data combined with diaries and focus groups to measure the effects of the different types of instruction. Results show that learners perceived instruction in this area to be useful for conversations they needed to have and that in tests there was a significant short-term effect on use of the target discourse markers for the PPP group when compared to the III group and a control. This was not sustained into a delayed test eight weeks later. This may have been due to a similar problem found by Dörnyei (1995) which was discussed previously. Jones and Carter (2014) used a free constructed response test, meaning participants could avoid using the target discourse markers if they chose to. Jones and Cleary (2019) investigated the use of ellipsis, as part of a study into the effectiveness of using dramatised literature in instruction on spoken language. Participants were divided into three groups, with two experimental groups receiving instruction based on the various aspects of spoken language in the videos, including ellipsis. Both groups received explicit instruction, but one group had their texts enhanced to highlight the ellipsis. Experimental groups were compared via receptive post- and delayed tests with each other and a control group receiving no instruction. Results from the gains made at the pre- to post-test and pre- to delayed test stages showed significantly better results for the experimental group using enhanced texts when compared to the control group. This shows that instruction can enhance awareness of such features.

Taken together, all of the studies discussed show the potential that conversation strategy instruction based on analysis of spoken corpus data has. Many studies also indicate the benefits of mixed-methods designs by using quantitative measures such as tests alongside learner questionnaires or interviews to measure perceptions of the usefulness of instruction. There is, however, a clear lack of studies focused specifically on the kind of conversation strategies described.

The aim of this study is therefore to offer one example of such a study in an ESL context. In doing so, I sought to answer the following research questions:

RQ1. To what extent does explicit instruction of conversation strategies enhance participants' ability to recognise them when used by others?

RQ2. To what extent does explicit instruction of conversation strategies enhance participants' ability to use them?

RQ3. To what extent do participants themselves perceive conversation strategies as useful tools to develop more successful conversations outside of class?

Methodology

As mentioned in the chapter introduction, a mixed-methods design was employed. The main part of the research took the form of an experimental study, with participants assigned to either an experimental ($N = 16$) or control group ($N = 14$). Each group took the following pre-tests: a receptive test and free constructed response test (hereafter the production test), in the form of a paired, interactive discussion task. The receptive test required participants to listen and read a conversation and identify language used to realise particular strategies (such as '*uh-huh*' – to show you are listening), while the discussion task gave opportunities to use strategies but did not force them to do so. Following the pre-test, the experimental group then received ten hours of instruction on conversation strategies over two weeks, while the control group did not. See the procedure section for details of the instruction. Subsequent to this, an equivalent receptive and production test was given to all participants – the test was in the same format, but the actual items were changed (see appendix 4A for samples).

The experimental group were also asked to keep a learning diary during the two weeks of teaching and four weeks after the instruction. This was structured and participants were given a template to follow, asking them to describe conversations they had, difficulties they had, any strategies used and the extent to which they thought these may have helped them. They were required to complete one entry per week. The aim of the diaries was to try and understand, from the participants' viewpoint, the extent to which they could recall and use the strategies taught and the extent to which they felt they felt that this helped them to develop more successful conversations. As mentioned above, this method was chosen because it is important to measure how learners perceive the effectiveness of instruction, as there is little chance that instruction will be successful without some level of learner 'buy in.' Diary data of this kind has been widely used in second language research to understand both learner and teacher viewpoints. It can give us access to introspective data which we may not be able to obtain through other qualitative methods such as observation (Bailey & Ochsner, 1983). For this reason, Nunan (1992, p. 118) describes diary studies as "important introspective tools" in qualitative research, as they allow us to understand aspects such as learner perception of instruction. In this case, it would have been both impossible and unethical for participants to record conversations they had outside of class and so recalling conversations and reflecting upon them was a more realistic way of obtaining this data.

Participants

Participants consisted of thirty students of mixed nationality, assigned to either an experimental group ($N = 16$) or a control group ($N = 14$), drawn from two language centres in the north west of England. All participants were at CEFR B1 level, based on placement tests undertaken in each institution. Broadly, a learner at this level, is said to have the following competences:

> Can understand the main points of clear standard input on familiar matters regularly encountered in work, school, leisure, etc. Can deal with most situations likely to arise whilst travelling in an area where the language is spoken. Can produce simple connected text on topics which are familiar or of personal interest. Can describe experiences and events, dreams, hopes & ambitions and briefly give reasons and explanations for opinions and plans.

(Council of Europe, 2020, Table 1)

In terms of the specific conversational ability, a learner is said to have the following competences:

> Can enter unprepared into conversations on familiar topics. Can follow clearly articulated speech directed at him/her in everyday conversation, though will sometimes have to ask for repetition of particular words and phrases. Can maintain a conversation or discussion but may sometimes be difficult to follow when trying to say exactly what he/she would like to. Can express and respond to feelings such as surprise, happiness, sadness, interest and indifference.

(Council of Europe, 2018, p. 85)

Naturally, any learner who tests as being at this level, may have these competences to a greater or lesser degree and will not have mastered them all. Such descriptors simply give a broad brush understanding of learners' levels, expressed in functional terms. They show us what learners can be expected to do with language rather than each specific item of language they will use to realise each function.

Participants had a range of L1s and consisted of the following nationalities: Chinese (4), Colombian (2) French (2), Italian (2), Japanese (1), Korean (6), Saudi Arabian (11), Spanish (1) and Venezuelan (1). Sixteen were male and fourteen were female. The mean age of participants was 24.9 years old and the ages ranged from 18–58. The mean length of prior English study was 5.9 years, ranging from three months to twelve years.

The sample used here was purposive, in that respondents had to be CEFR B1 level (as decided by placement tests) and there was also an intention to sample a range of nationalities. This aspect of the sample was largely based on convenience (which learners were available and willing to volunteer at the time of the study) but nine different nationalities were represented across the two groups, giving a good range. All participants were living and studying in the UK at the time of the study and thus had opportunities to interact in English outside of class time.

Procedure

Pre-tests were first given to all participants, with the production test followed by the receptive test. Participants were then tested again after two weeks, during which time the experimental group received instruction. Although a study of this type should ideally contain a delayed test, this was made impossible due to COVID-19 restrictions. Many participants returned to their different home countries and were unavailable or impossible to contact. The tests aimed to understand how students could recognise the strategies when used by others and how they could make use of them in a short speaking task. As mentioned, this meant that for the receptive test, participants listened to a dialogue while reading a transcript and identified language used to fulfil particular given strategies. The production test entailed a simple paired discussion task, which lasted approximately ten minutes per pair. Students were each given a choice of two similar topics, such as the following:

Student A: Tell your partner about a good OR bad meal you have had

Student B: Listen and ask your partner any questions you would like to ask.

Once the first topic was discussed, students swapped roles and a different topic was given. Topics were deliberately general and considered to be within students' abilities and were changed from pre- to post-test. Each test was recorded and following this, the number of correct uses of the language taught for each strategy were counted and categorised under the four main areas of strategies identified by McCarthy and McCarten (2018): showing listenership, managing the conversation, managing your own turn as a whole and taking account of others. These uses were then added together to create an overall score for each group.

The potential issue with using a production test of this nature is of course that students may not use the target forms at all, something discussed previously in relation to other studies such as Dörnyei (1995). This may simply mean that the test allows for avoidance of the target forms. However, on balance, it was felt that the discussion task used did provide opportunities to use the strategies taught and this was the most realistic way to understand the participants' ability to use them spontaneously and to assess their ability to produce them. The receptive tests aimed to assess participants' declarative knowledge, based on whether they could recognise language used to fulfil common strategies.

Following the tests, the experimental group were then given ten hours of instruction by a colleague working at a language centre. Lesson content was designed together via discussion of student needs and instruction was arranged to cover and recycle the four main categories of conversation strategies mentioned previously and based on McCarthy and McCarten (2018): showing listenership, managing the conversation as a whole, managing your own turn and taking account of others. Examples of the kind of language taught for each broad strategy and samples of how these were broken down can be seen in Table 4.1 (see appendix 4B for everything taught).

Table 4.1

Samples of Conversation Strategy Instruction

Strategy	Sub-strategy	Sample language taught to realise the strategy
Showing listenership	Showing you have had a similar experience	*Yeah, that happened to me, I know what you mean*
Managing the conversation as a whole	Dealing with interruptions and returning to your topic	*(anyway) As I was/you were saying, Now where was I?*
Managing your own turn	Starting a new topic	*So, right*
Taking account of others	Using vague language to describe things and interests	*And things like that…all kinds of stuff*

Although each strategy was covered, more weight and time were given to listenership than the others, as it was felt to be an area which learners at this level needed and could easily be recycled across a number of classes. The language used to exemplify each strategy was informed by the kinds of spoken corpus research discussed in chapters 1 and 2. O'Keeffe et al. (2007), for example, show that '*I mean*' is the second most frequent two-word lexical chunk used in the five million word CANCODE corpus of spoken British English and chapter two shows that '*stuff*' is commonly also used in conversations by ELF users.

Lessons were explicit in the sense that learners were told which strategies they were focusing on and the aim of each class was made clear to them. Each strategy was described in simple functional terms to learners, e.g., showing you are interested when listening. Lessons were taught using a broad communicative methodology, with both published and authentic material used. The lessons took various shapes but drew upon principles common to communicative language teaching in general. These can be summarised as follows:

1. Language was explored in context.
2. Learners were guided towards understanding meaning and form by inductive means, such as teacher questions and exercises. This aims to foster noticing habits amongst learners. As mentioned in previous chapters, this belief, after Schmidt (1990, 2010), is that conscious registration of form(s) within the input can help learners to convert form(s) into intake when they encounter them and that this increases the possibility that they will be able to use such forms, should they choose to.
3. Practice of the language was given in various ways; both in meaningful activities and in more controlled ways.

This did not mean all classes were organised in the same way – there were, for example, lessons which employed the type of task-based framework described by Willis (1998) and classes which drew upon the Illustration-Interaction-Induction (III) principles of McCarthy and McCarten (2018). As a reminder, these principles can be summarised as they were in the previous chapters using this slightly edited excerpt from McCarthy and McCarten (2018, p. 12)

Illustration	Conversational extracts are chosen to exemplify a given feature *in context*, supported by corpus evidence, even if the extracts are edited versions of original corpus texts. A single sentence or series of sentences will never truly suffice.
Interaction	This is itself a form of practice. The practice generated is aimed at fostering the habit of interacting with texts, noticing and apprehending key features and using them in the contexts in which they normally occur.
Induction	The practice of awareness skills offers a critical support for this stage, which is a process of incorporating new knowledge into existing knowledge and apprehending underlying principles, whether those principles be formal rules of lexico-grammar or socio-culturally-determined conventions of conversational behaviour.

As in chapter 3, the principles of III were not employed as lesson steps or stages. An example of how lessons worked in practice can be shown in Extract 1 below, which gives a sample procedure used in one lesson.

Extract 1. Sample lesson procedure.

1. Warmer - think of interesting/enjoyable things you can do where you live.
2. Prepare to tell someone about something you have done recently which was interesting or enjoyable. Help with lexis as needed.
3. Students work in pairs to tell each other about what was interesting/enjoyable.
   The outcome should be to find 3 similarities or differences in their stories.
   Get feedback on similarities/differences.
4. Demo the same task with a student and this time you show listenership to show a) you are following and b) interested and c) empathetic. Students listen and note how the language you use is different to theirs. They should notice the listenership.
5. Check why this is important.
6. Categorise listenership phrases into three: a) you can understand, b) you are interested and c) you have had a similar experience e.g.

   A) *Right, yeah, uh huh.*
   B) *That's interesting, Really? Wow!*
   C) *I bet, Yeah, that happened to me, I know what you mean.*

7. Practice – you say something e.g., 'I just bumped into (famous person that they will know)' and they must pick a good response e.g., Wow! Drill each response after it is elicited to get good stress and intonation.
8. Students do the same in pairs.
9. Tell another person your interesting/enjoyable experience and put the expressions on cards. Each student picks three cards.

They have to try and use them in the task, which is a repeat of 3.

This sample procedure shows that the strategy is contextualised within a conversation (in this case, a simple task with a simple outcome). The same context is then used for inductive discovery of the listenership used and to help students notice it in a better model of the task they have just completed. They are then given further opportunities to practise the language in both mechanical and more meaningful ways, in this case via a simple repetition of the first task undertaken.

Diaries

Participants in the experimental group were asked to keep a simple learning diary for a total of six weeks: two weeks during the instruction and four weeks afterwards. This diary took the form of a simple template and learners submitted this online, once a week. The prompts used were as follows:

Describe a conversation you had this week (where / why / who with / how did you feel?)

Which strategy/ies did you use?

Describe how using the strategy affected your ability to have a successful conversation.

If you could have the same conversation again, describe what you would do differently.

What kind of conversation would you like to practise next week? *For example: General conversation with friends / discussing your area of study or work / in a shop, doctors, hairdressers...*

Which strategies might be useful to help you communicate in this conversation?

These prompts were designed to help the students to write each diary entry easily and also to encourage reflection and noticing of their use (or non-use) of conversation strategies. Naturally, when we solicit diaries such as this from learners, there is a possibility that learners may not truly reflect on how they felt but attempt to write what they think the researcher wants, knowing these would be read. This is certainly a potential weakness but of course, the same could be said of many qualitative methods. There is always potential in interviews, for example, that participants will simply say what they think you want to hear. This risk cannot be fully countered but if we wish to obtain introspective data such as this, it is a risk we have to take.

The second potential weakness is that asking learners to write a diary in English at this level may be challenging. This is why a template was provided. This did not remove the difficulty of writing the diary in the L2 but it offered essential guidance to learners. This also countered a third weakness of diaries. Dörnyei (2007) and Bolger et al. (2003) note that diaries demand a lot from the participants in terms of their time and commitment and this can mean that participation gradually tails off over the course of a study. The template was fairly simple to complete and diaries were also collected at regular intervals to ensure learners were participating. A final problem is one which several researchers have noted; the data is difficult to analyse objectively (Dörnyei, 2007). Should the data be analysed subjectively, it could lead to us finding only what we are hoping to find and not what the data actually tells us. In this study I attempted to overcome by using NVivo software (QSR, 2020) to help with analysis. See the next section for more details.

Data analysis

The test data was analysed using SPSS (IBM, 2020) Initial normality checks were undertaken and revealed that the data were not normally distributed. As a result, test results were analysed using the non-parametric, Mann Whitney U test to compare each group at the pre-and post-test stages. This is considered broadly equivalent to an independent samples t-test and can be used with non-parametric data when comparing two groups. Overall means and gains made from pre- to post-test were compared and effect sizes calculated where significant differences were found between the groups. Pearson's r was chosen as the measurement of effect size, with 0.1 considered a small effect, 0.3 a medium effect and 0.5 and above a large effect (Cohen,

1988). Effect sizes are important as they tell us how big the difference is between two groups' scores and not simply that they are significantly different. A significant difference in scores with a large effect size, for example, suggests a stronger effect for instruction than a small effect size. In addition, comparisons were made between particular categories of strategies used.

NVivo (QSR, 2020) software was used to sort and code the diary data. As mentioned in chapter 3, Computer-Assisted Qualitative Data Analysis Software (CAQDAS) software was chosen as it offers a greater level of objectivity than manual coding. CAQDAS software allows us to approach coding in a way which is more systematic and thus more objective than manual coding, creating categories and moving around the data with ease. These codes can then also be checked using such tools as word frequency to ensure they accurately represent the views expressed in the data. This frequency data supports the ways in which we might categorise the data, adding a systematic and objective dimension to the analysis.

As the diaries all followed a template, answers were more restricted than the open-ended questions used to survey teachers in chapter 3. For this reason, the themes I chose to focus on were related to the template. These were:

Kinds of conversations students had and wished to have

Strategies used

The extent to which strategies helped

The strategies they would like to use

Results and discussion

In order to discuss the results, each research question will be considered in turn.

RQ1. To what extent does explicit instruction of conversation strategies enhance participants' ability to recognise them when used by others?

Table 4.2 gives the descriptive statistics (means and standard deviations) for the receptive pre- and post-tests.

Table 4.2

Descriptive Statistics for Receptive Pre- and Post-Tests

	Pre-test Mean (SD)	Post-test Mean (SD)
Experimental group (N = 16)	4.00 (2.68)	6.37 (2.72)
Control group (N = 14)	4.29 (2.16)	4.14 (2.79)
Total (N = 30)	4.13 (2.41)	5.33 (2.94)

Note: Maximum mark = 11

Comparison of means shows no significant differences between the groups at the pre-test stage (p = .721), which shows that the two groups had a similar level of receptive knowledge prior to instruction, something the means clearly indicate. At the post-test stage, the overall scores show that the experimental group performed significantly better than the control with a medium effect size (Mann Whitney U = 64.5, Wilcoxon W = 169.50, Z = -1.98, p = .047, r = 0.36). When the pre-test to post-test gain scores are compared, this result is highly significant, with a large effect size (Mann Whitney U = 29.0, Wilcoxon W = 134.0, Z = -3.848, p <.001, r = 0.63). This demonstrates that the instruction was highly effective (in the short term) in increasing participants' ability to recognise conversation strategies and common language used to realise them. Although the control group participants were in an English-speaking environment, there was no gain made from pre- to post-test, suggesting that this awareness did not develop only from interaction in English inside or outside class, at least for the duration of this study. The kind of declarative knowledge developed by the experimental group (the ability to recognise language used for particular conversation strategies in a sample conversation) does not of course guarantee they will then be able to make use of this in their own language production. However, there is a long-held view that there is at least an interface between conscious awareness of language and its acquisition (e.g., Schmidt, 1990; Sharwood Smith, 1981) and as mentioned in previous chapters, this has been supported by a great deal of research into the noticing hypothesis (e.g., Indrarathne & Kormos, 2017; Rosa & O'Neill, 1999; Shekary & Tahririan, 2006). The significantly improved

114

scores of the experimental group on this receptive test could certainly contribute to this noticing.

RQ2. To what extent does explicit instruction of conversation strategies enhance participants' ability to use them?

Table 4.3 gives the descriptive statistics (means and standard deviations) for the production pre- and post-tests.

Table 4.3

Descriptive Statistics for Production Pre- and Post-Tests

	Pre-test Mean (SD)	Post-test Mean (SD)
Experimental group (N = 16)	6.93 (4.46)	11.12 (4.19)
Control group (N = 14)	4.78 (4.20)	5.07 (3.58)
Total (N = 30)	5.93 (4.40)	8.30 (5.27)

Note: No maximum score

Comparison of means shows no significant differences between the groups at the pre-test stage (p = .161), which again shows that prior to instruction the two groups had a similar level of ability in regard to use of the conversation strategies.

At the post- test stage, the overall scores show that the experimental group performed significantly better than the control with a large effect size (Mann Whitney U = 32.5, Wilcoxon W = 137.50, Z = -3.31, p = .001, r = 0.6). When the pre-test to post-test gain scores are compared, this result is also significant with a medium effect size (Mann Whitney U = 65.0, Wilcoxon W = 170.0, Z = -1.96, p = .05, r = 0.35). This demonstrates that the instruction was effective (in the short term) in increasing participants' ability to use at least some of the conversation strategies and common language used to realise them. The results are not quite as positive as for the receptive test but to some extent, this is to be expected when employing a production test of this nature. As discussed, there is a chance that learners will simply avoid using some of what has been taught. Nevertheless, the

115

results show that instruction can have a positive short-term effect on the learners' ability to use these strategies.

It is also worth examining the overall scores for each type of strategy (listenership, managing the conversation as a whole, managing your own turn and taking account of others)

Tables 4.4 and 4.5 give the descriptive statistics (means and standard deviations) for this data at the pre- and post- test stage.

Table 4.4

Descriptive Statistics for Each Strategy Area – Production Pre-Test

Pre-test Mean (SD)	Listenership	Managing the conversation	Managing your turn	Taking account of others
Experimental group (N = 16)	3.43 (3.75)	.00 (.00)	3.31 (2.72)	.18 (.54)
Control group (N = 14)	1.71 (2.61)	.07 (.26)	2.92 (3.07)	.07 (.26)
Total (N = 30)	2.63 (3.33)	.03 (.18)	3.13 (2.84)	.13 (.43)

Table 4.5

Descriptive Statistics for Each Strategy Area – Production Post-Test

Pre-test Mean (SD)	Listenership	Managing the conversation	Managing your turn	Taking account of others
Experimental group (N = 16)	5.75 (4.52)	.43 (1.50)	4.62 (3.07)	.31 (.47)
Control group (N = 14)	1.71 (1.43)	.00 (.00)	2.71 (2.94)	.64 (1.59)
Total (N =30)	3.86 (3.96)	.23 (1.10)	3.73 (3.11)	.46 (1.13)

This data shows clearly that both groups made much greater use of listenership and managing your own turn than the two other strategies. When these areas are compared at the post- test stage, the only strategy area which was used significantly more by the experimental group was the overall listenership score, (Mann Whitney $U = 39.5$, Wilcoxon $W = 144.50$, $Z = -3.05$, $p = 002$). This shows that the significant gains made at the post-test stage were mainly due to a greatly increased use of this strategy, although, as noted, the use of managing your own turn also increased. To some extent this may reflect the greater amount of attention paid to listenership in the instruction. It may also reflect the focus of many students at B1 level on either responding to others or focusing on their own turn, a finding made by Jones et al. (2018) in relation to successful spoken learner language. Showing you are listening or interested can be achieved with a simple word or short phrase while you are focused on someone else's turn. On the other hand, taking account of others or managing the whole conversation are likely to be more demanding strategies for learners at this level. They require learners to consider what they wish to say at the same time as considering such things as whether their conversation partner knows a place they are talking about (*'do you know x?'*) or that they wish to close a topic. For these reasons, perhaps we can expect learners at this level to recognise such strategies but not yet use them consistently. Or perhaps they simply need a longer time to recognise, understand and practise such strategies, something a delayed test might have captured. Having said this, there is no doubt that strategies such as listenership are useful and necessary to help oil the wheels of conversation. As such, they are likely to help learners to have the kind of conversations envisaged in the CEFR descriptor for this level and beyond that.

RQ3. To what extent do participants themselves perceive conversation strategies as useful tools to develop more successful conversations outside of class?

As described in the methodology section, the way the diary data was categorised was based on the template participants were given. I will look at sample comments for each theme and then discuss what all the themes tell us in relation to research question 3. For each sample from learner diaries, names of people and places have been removed and replaced with 'X' to protect anonymity. English use has not been corrected.

Kinds of conversations students had and would like to have

What is clear from the data is that the participants had a mixture of transactional and interpersonal conversations, both inside and outside of class. This shows the value of being in an English-speaking environment, enabling students to have conversations with a mixture of native and non-native speakers, using English as a common language. Some examples of this are as follows:

- *I had a conversation with the receptionist in my accommodation, because I had a problem with the lighting in my room.*
- *Today I had conversation with my friend. We met each other in a coffee shop we talked about studying here.*
- *Last week I had a conversation with my classmate in the class. We were talking about our plan in the weekend.*
- *I talked with X at a share kitchen in my accommodation.*
- *I had a conversation with the reception at the accommodation about the key.*
- *I made a conversation with someone at the gym asked him about his workout.*
- *This week I had a conversation with a Japanese girl whose name is X. The conversation happened on our way to X when we were on the train.*
- *Last week, I had a conversation with my classmate on our way to another classroom.*

It was also interesting to see that some participants counted text-chat as conversations. Given that there are many similarities and overlaps with face-to-face conversation, this is probably no surprise but does perhaps have potential implications for how we teach and practise conversation strategies, something I will return to in the concluding chapter of this book.

- *This week I texting with X. I met her in drawing class last week and I want to ask about London.*

The topics of these conversations varied but were often on the kind of familiar, everyday topics described in the CEFR conversation descriptor for this level, such as sport, food or films. The transactional conversations were connected to simple things participants needed such as bank cards or help in their accommodation.

- *I had a fantastic conversation about last match for X club, it was in coffee with my friends.*
- *Today we talked about disgusting foods.*
- *I had a fantastic conversation about last movie I have watch.*
- *I had a conversation with the receptionist about our lift.*
- *I had a conversation with the manager of restaurant, because the food was not good enough.*
- *This week I had a conversation with a salesclerk in Boots, since I need her help.*

The conversations participants wished to have included a similar range of transactional and interpersonal conversations, on a range of familiar topics. Samples of these topics included the following:

- *Discussing your area of study or work.*
- *General conversation in a shop, doctors, hairdressers.*
- *More practice with my friends, and also I have to call at post office.*
- *If I buy something, I want to ask about the product with no error.*
- *I'd like to talk about Christmas.*
- *About something that show interest of studying in X.*
- *Meet someone at the café.*
- *I'd like to have conversation with doctor so I can ask him about the medicine.*
- *I'd like to conversation about eating habits.*

While many of the topics students did talk about and would like to talk about would be covered in standard course materials, it is notable that none of the participants mentioned the kind of topics regularly featured as discussions in textbooks and exams, such as the environment, tourism, technology and so on. For these participants at least, the kinds of conversations they had were on more straightforward (and less 'worthy') topics.

Strategies used

It is clear from the diary data that most participants reported using conversation strategies both inside and outside of classes. The most common strategies they reported using were connected to listenership, something which reflects the greater use of this strategy in the test results. This is shown in word frequency analysis for this theme. Excluding proper nouns, articles and prepositions, the frequency count shows 'following' as the second most frequent word and 'response' as the seventh most frequent word. Examples of learner comments are as follows:

- *I used responses that is following.*
- *And I used conversation strategies that appeared I followed and listen her.*
- *I used conversation strategies that appear I follow my friend.*
- *Showing I am response in something good.*
- *Response to something good and response to something bad strategies.*
- *Some comment as that's fascinating, wow, gorgeous work*
- *When I understood his sentence, I said "Uh huh, Wow, I understand"*
- *So I used strategies like right, yeah, I know what you mean.*

Learners also mention use of other strategies they had been taught and the use of other more generalised strategies and language. Examples of these comments are as follows:

- *We showed pictures which is our uniforms, when we talked.*
- *Through the conversation, I tried to ask more questions about the festival.*
- *I used a variety of adjectives.*
- *The strategies that show I have has a similar experience and giving myself time to think.*
- *I used key word strategy, eye contact, and body language*
- *I used relative pronouns.*
- *I use following strategy, show my interest, use interrupting strategy.*

Overall, the comments are encouraging, as they show that learners could often recall strategies taught and report that they made use of them. As discussed in relation to the test results, the common use of different forms of listenership probably reflects the greater weighting this was given in the teaching but also because this is likely to be easier to employ at this level.

The extent to which strategies were perceived to help

Learners' comments showed that in general they perceived the strategies they used to be helpful. The comments in this regard showed they felt they could help in terms of developing what they wished to say but they also demonstrated an awareness of how strategies could help the conversations as a whole. Typical comments are as follows:

- *It shows the other that we are interested in the conversation and it makes the conversation long.*
- *The person who I spoke with was interested too.*
- *The first thing is that, I feel I can manage the conversation and show understanding.*
- *I think it is very useful when I don't remember any words, and person who have conversation with me is more like me.*
- *It made interesting conversation.*
- *These helped me tell her news.*
- *I think these led to a deeper conversation.*
- *I used the 'response to something good,' they were very satisfied.*
- *It helps to understand other peoples word more clearly.*

Such comments are pleasing because they show some awareness of the interpersonal role of conversation strategies, alongside how they can help to develop what learners themselves wish to say. Strategies such as listenership have an interpersonal role to play and are not just designed to help an individual speaker but rather to help the wider goal of more fluent conversation between speakers. As McCarthy and McCarten (2018, p. 25) state "the goals of conversational practice are fluency, confluence and successful social interaction."

The strategies they would like to use

Many of the strategies which participants stated they could use in future conversations reflected the most common strategy taught and indeed uses in the post-test: listenership. There was also some limited awareness shown of strategies which students did not employ often in the post-tests, one being the use of vague language or items such as *'you know X?'* to take account of the listener. Examples of the comments are as follows:

- *Using vague language and interrupting politely.*
- *Using vague language.*
- *I think response strategies is useful. like 'That's interesting, I bet, No way!'.*
- *I always say That's interesting or Really? This things are very useful and I'll effort to use you know..?, What do you call it/them?*
- *Response and echoing and say 'fantastic,' 'awesome!'*
- *I think that might be 'You are following.'*

Overall, the diary data reinforces the test data to a large degree. It is clear that participants reported that they could make use of some of the strategies taught in conversations outside of class. They could recall what had been taught and make clear how it had been used in a conversation they had. In general, they also perceived the instruction to have been useful in helping them to have more successful spoken interaction. The types of conversations they had also show a range of transactional and interpersonal goals, mainly centred on simple everyday topics such as buying things in shops, talking about sport or their studies. The most common strategy type they reported using was listenership, as was shown in the post-test data. Participants showed a clear awareness that such strategies help them to manage their own turns but also have a positive effect on the conversation as a whole.

Conclusion

This chapter has described a mixed-methods experimental study, comparing the short-term effects of instruction on receptive and productive knowledge of conversation strategies. The results were based on a receptive and a production test and supplemented with learner diaries. Test results show significant short-term effects for the experimental group when compared to the control group and diary data confirms that participants found the instruction useful and could employ some conversation strategies in classes and outside of them. There was a prevalence of listenership strategies used in both tests and reported in diaries and much less use of strategies to manage the conversation or take account of others. This can be accounted for by a combination of the emphasis on listenership in the instruction and the participants' level. Overall, the results are positive because they show that instruction in this area can have a clear short-term effect on learners' abilities to use and recognise conversation strategies. Learners in the control group did not appear to simply pick up these strategies from standard classes and interactions in the ESL environment. This suggests that targeted instruction in this area is likely to be needed to at least speed up the rate at which conversation strategies and the language to realise them can be learnt.

Despite these positive results, there are obvious limitations to this study. The first is that the sample size is relatively small. Future studies would ideally include greater numbers of participants at the same level of language competence or above. The second limitation is that there was no delayed test, as COVID-19 restrictions meant that a number of participants were not available. This means that the test results only show the short-term effect of the instruction. The inclusion of a delayed test would have provided a measure of the longer-term effects of the instruction on both groups. There is no real consensus regarding the optimal amount of time after a study to hold a delayed test, but Schmitt (2010) has suggested a delay of at least two weeks after instruction is ideal, while Truscott (1998) suggests that a delay of more than five weeks but less than one year is ideal. In recent years, many experimental studies of a similar design to this have employed delayed tests of between three weeks and five months (e.g., Fordyce, 2014; Halenko, 2018; Jones & Cleary, 2019) so any delay of three weeks or more would seem to be ideal, depending on the availability of participants. Another limitation is that the context of this study was an ESL environment, which was in many ways ideal for language acquisition. Participants were multilingual, meaning there was a need to use English as a common language in classes and there were many opportunities for face-to-face conversations outside of class, as attested in the learner diaries. This simply means we cannot generalise these results to all contexts and monolingual EFL contexts may differ substantially. Further similar studies in EFL and other ESL contexts would be useful to replicate these results.

Appendix 4A Sample test items used

Receptive test

Listen to the conversation and read the transcript. Two friends are talking about a lesson they had.
Find and <u>write</u> words or phrases from the conversation which show the following conversation strategies and write these next to each strategy.

Example:
Showing you want to greet someone: *hello*
    1. Showing you are listening and understanding =
    2. Showing you want to go back to something said earlier =

Transcript

A. So, can you remember a good or bad lesson you had?
B. Well, it's tricky err…to remember good lessons! I can definitely remember a really bad lesson!
A. Uh huh.
B. Yeah, it was in Bangkok while I was trying to learn Thai.
A. Right.
B. Basically, the teacher made it impossible to learn. I mean, not impossible but really, really difficult.
A. Really??? Wow! Why was that?
B. Well, we had to memorise a lot of random vocabulary in a really short time and that's sort of impossible. Another thing was that we then had a test on this vocabulary. It was very easy to fail!
A. Yeah, I can imagine.
B. I think you can learn a bit if it is connected to something but this was really long list of different words. Anyway, what about you? Have you got an experience like this that you can remember?
A. Er, well, as you said, it's, you know, it's easy to remember bad lessons! I can remember some awful French lessons at school, but it is hard to remember just one!

Production test (conducted in pairs, with roles then reversed and topics changed)

Student A
Tell your partner about:
A good or bad meal you have had. Your partner will listen and ask questions.

Student B
Listen to your partner and ask them questions about their story.

Appendix 4B - Instruction

Strategy	Sub-strategy	Sample language taught to realise the strategy
Showing listenership	Showing you have had a similar experience	*Yeah, that happened to me, I know what you mean, I bet*
	Showing you are following	*Right, Yeah, Uh huh, Got it*
	Showing you are interested (response to something good)	*That's interesting/fantastic/amazing/incredible/amazing*
	Showing you are interested (response to something bad)	*Wow! Really? Great!*
		Oh no! Oh dear That's/how terrible/awful
	Showing you are interested (but want to show disbelief)	*I can't believe it! No way! No! That's incredible*
Managing the conversation as a whole	Dealing with interruptions and returning to the topic	*(anyway) As I was/you were saying, Now where was I?, Excuse me, I haven't finished, Hang on a minute, Okay then*
	Interrupting politely	*Actually, can I just say…, Excuse me, may I interrupt, Can I just point out that, Actually, that's not true*
Managing your own turn	Opening a new topic	*So, right*
	Giving yourself time to think	*Well, gimme a minute, just a sec, I mean, erm*
Taking account of others	Using vague language to describe things and interests	*And things/stuff like that, all kinds of stuff/things, all types of…, all sorts of…, and everything*
	Checking the listener can follow	*You know X? You know?*
	Trying to remember words	*What do you call it/ them? What's his/her/its name?*

References

Bailey, K., & Ochsner, R. (1983). A methodological view of diary studies: Windmill tilting or social science? In J. Richards, & D. Nunan (Eds.), *Second language teacher education* (pp. 251–256). Cambridge University Press.

Mackey, A., & Goo, J. (2007). Interaction research in SLA: A meta-analysis and research synthesis. In A. Mackey (Ed.), *Conversational interaction and second language acquisition*, (pp. 407–450). Oxford University Press.

Bolger, N., Davis, A., & Rafaeli, E. (2003). Diary methods: Capturing life as it is lived. *Annual Review of Psychology, 54*, 579–616. https://doi.org/10.1146/annurev.psych.54.101601.145030

Boulton, A., & Cobb, T (2017) Corpus use in language learning: A meta-analysis. *Language Learning, 67*(2), 348–393. https://doi.org/10.1111/lang.12224

Carrier, K. A. (2003) Improving high school English language learners' second language listening through strategy instruction. *Bilingual Research Journal, 27*(3), 283–408. https://doi.org/10.1080/15235882.2003.10162600

Chen, A-h. (2009). Listening strategy instruction: Exploring Taiwanese college students' strategy development. *Asian EFL Journal, 11*(2), 54–85. https://www.asian-efl-journal.com/main-editions-new/listening-strategy-instruction-exploring-taiwanese-college-students-strategy-development/

Cohen, L., Manion, L., & Morrison, K. (2007). *Research methods in education.* Routledge.

Council of Europe (2018). *Common European framework of reference for languages: Learning, teaching, assessment companion volume with new descriptors.* https://rm.coe.int/cefr-companion-volume-with-new-descriptors-2018/1680787989

Council of Europe (2020). *Global scale common reference levels.* https://www.coe.int/en/web/common-european-framework-reference-languages/table-1-cefr-3.3-common-reference-levels-global-scale

Diepenbroek, L., & Derwing, T. (2014). To what extent do popular ESL textbooks incorporate oral fluency and pragmatic development. *TESL Canada Journal, 30*(7), 1.

https://doi.org/10.18806/tesl.v30i7.1149

Dörnyei, Z. (2007). *Research methods in applied linguistics*. Oxford University Press.

Dörnyei, Z. (1995). On the teachability of communication strategies. *TESOL Quarterly, 29*(1), 55–85. https://doi.org/10.2307/3587805

Fordyce, K. (2014). The differential effects of explicit and implicit instruction on EFL learners' use of epistemic stance, *Applied Linguistics, 35*(1), 6–28. https://doi.org/10.1093/applin/ams076

Gunning, P., & Oxford, R. (2014). Children's learning strategy use and the effects of strategy instruction on success in learning ESL in Canada. *System, 43*(1), 82–100. https://doi.org/10.1016/j.system.2013.12.012

Halenko, N. (2018). Using computer-assisted language learning (CALL) tools to enhance output practice. In C. Jones (Ed.), *Practice in second language learning* (pp. 137–163). Cambridge University Press.

IBM Corp. [Computer software]. (2020.) *IBM SPSS statistics for Windows, version 27.0*. IBM Corp.

Indrarathne, B., & Kormos, J. (2017). Attentional processing of input in explicit and implicit learning conditions: an eye-tracking study. *Studies in Second Language Acquisition, 39*(3), 401–430. https://doi.org/10.1017/S027226311600019X

Jones, C., & Carter, R. (2014). Teaching spoken discourse markers explicitly: A comparison of III and PPP. *International Journal of English Studies, 14*(1), 37–54. https://doi.org/10.6018/ijes/14/1/161001

Jones, C., & Cleary, J. (2019). Literature, TV drama and spoken language awareness. In C. Jones (Ed.), *Literature, spoken language and speaking skills in second language learning* (pp. 66–95). Cambridge University Press.

Jones, C., Byrne, S., & Halenko, N. (2018). *Successful spoken English: Findings from learner corpora*. Routledge.

Kelle, U. (2002). Computer-assisted qualitative data analysis. In C. Seale, G. Gobo, J. F. Gubrium, & D. Silverman (Eds.), *Qualitative research practice* (pp. 473–489). Sage Publications.

Lam, W. K. (2010). Implementing communication strategy Instruction in the ESL oral classroom: What do low-proficiency learners tell us? *TESL Canada Journal, 27*(2), 11–30. https://doi.org/10.18806/tesl.v27i2.1056

McCarthy, M., & Carter, R. (1995). Spoken grammar: What is it and how can we teach it? *ELT Journal, 49*(3), 207–218. https://doi.org/10.1093/elt/49.3.207

McCarthy, M., & McCarten, J. (2018). Now you're talking! Practising conversation in second language learning. In C. Jones (Ed.), *Practice in second language learning* (pp. 7–29). Cambridge University Press.

McCarthy, M., McCarten, J., & Sandiford, H. (2014). *Touchstone second edition, levels 1–4.* Cambridge University Press.

Nunan, D. (1992). *Research methods in language teaching.* Cambridge University Press.

O'Keeffe, A., McCarthy, M., & Carter, R. (2007). *From corpus to classroom.* Cambridge University Press.

QSR International Pty Ltd. [computer software]. (2020). *NVivo.* https://www.qsrinternational.com/nvivo-qualitative-data-analysis-software/home

Rosa, E., & O'Neill, M. (1999). Explicitness, intake and the issue of awareness: Another piece to the puzzle. *Studies in Second Language Acquisition, 21*(4), 511–566. http://dx.doi.org/10.1017/s0272263199004015

Scherer, A., & Wertheimer, M. (1964). *A psycholinguistic experiment in foreign language teaching.* McGraw Hill.

Siegel, J. (2013). Second language learners' perceptions of listening strategy instruction. *Innovation in language learning and teaching, 7*(1), 1–18. https://doi.org/10.1080/17501229.2011.653110

Sharwood Smith, M. (1981). Consciousness-raising and the second language learner. *Applied Linguistics, 2*(2), 159–168. https://doi.org/10.1093/applin/II.2.159

Schmitt, N. (2010). *Researching vocabulary: A vocabulary research manual.* Palgrave Macmillan.

Spada, N., & Tomita (2010). Interactions between type of instruction and type of language feature: A meta-analysis. *Language Learning, 60*(2), 263–308. https://doi.org/10.1111/j.1467-9922.2010.00562.x

Talandis, G., & Stout, M. (2015) Getting EFL students to speak: An action research approach. *ELT Journal*, *69*(1), 11–25. https://doi.org/10.1093/elt/ccu037

Taylor, G. (2002). Teaching gambits: The effect of task variation and instruction on the use of conversation strategies by intermediate Spanish students. *Foreign Language Annals*, *35*(2), 171–189. https://doi.org/10.1111/j.1944-9720.2002.tb03153.x

Timmis, I. (2005). Towards a framework for teaching spoken grammar. *ELT Journal*, *59*(2), 117–125. https://doi.org/10.1093/eltj/cci025

Truscott, J. (1998). Noticing in second language acquisition: a critical review. *Second Language Research*, *14*(2), 103–135. https://doi.org/10.1191/026765898674803209

Schmidt, R. W. (1990). The role of consciousness in second language learning. *Applied Linguistics*, *11*(2), 129–158. https://doi.org/10.1093/applin/11.2.129

Schmidt, R. W. (2010). Attention, awareness and individual differences in language learning. In W. M. Chan, S. Chi, K. N. Cin, J. Istanto, M. Nagami, J. W. Sew, T. Suthiwan., & I. Walker (Eds.), *Proceedings of CLaSIC 2010, Singapore, December 2-4* (pp. 721–737). University of Singapore Centre for Language Studies.

Shekary, M., & Tahririan, M. H. (2006). Negotiation of meaning and noticing in text-based online chat. *The Modern Language Journal*, *90*(4), 557–573. http://doi.org/10.1111/j.1540-4781.2006.00504.x

Wildner-Bassett, M. E. (1984). *Improving pragmatic aspects of learners' interlanguage*. Narr.

Willis, J. (1998). *A framework for task-based learning*. Longman.

CHAPTER 5

Study 4. Action Research Study in an EFL Context

Introduction

Chapter 4 focused on a mixed-methods study in an ESL context (the UK). As noted in previous chapters, it is also important to explore the effects of teaching these strategies in other contexts. This chapter attempts this within the EFL context of a university setting in Japan. Unlike the previous chapter, a different approach is taken here. In this case, qualitative research based on an action research model was employed to measure the effects of instruction over a one-month period, as perceived by learners themselves. Action research has been defined by Rust and Clark (2007, p. 4) as something undertaken by teachers "taking action to improve teaching and learning plus systematic study of the action and its consequences." In educational settings, this typically involves a set of steps including identifying an area we wish to research, planning a study, taking action, observing the results of this action and reflecting on the results. This is often viewed as a cyclical process in that a study is refined and developed to continually improve practice over time (Borg, 2016) so that the results of one individual cycle contribute to a continual process of development. The ultimate aim is to improve learning and teaching, although in other contexts such as healthcare, it may be used to develop conditions and practices for patients and staff (Koshy et al., 2010).

In this study, the cycle was adapted so that a difficulty was identified, a study planned, action taken in the form of instruction and the results then observed via diaries and interviews. The results are then reflected upon and implications drawn from them. As I was not the regular teacher of the students, the cycle was not repeated and further developed but it was hoped that the results would be useful for reflecting on practices in this and other similar contexts. Studies of this nature allow us to view learning from the perspective of the learner and give us a chance to consider what the results might mean for teaching practice in a particular context and are increasingly common (Edwards & Burns, 2016). This reflection has implications

132

for teaching in this context but there may also be implications for other, similar, EFL contexts.

The area chosen to investigate was an often-reported issue amongst Japanese EFL learners: low confidence and ability in relation to conversational skills. While this is obviously not the case for all Japanese EFL learners, it is commonly reported that speaking skills are an area in need of attention (e.g., Cutrone, 2009; Mori, 2011; The (Japanese) Ministry of Education, Culture, Sports, Science and Technology (MEXT, 2014). As O'Sullivan (1992) identified some time ago, learners in Japan take compulsory EFL classes for a minimum of eight or nine years. These often start in junior high school but may also begin in primary school. Compulsory classes are also standard at universities in the first year. Although changes have been made so that communicative lessons are now a common part of school classes, many learners finish these with a larger amount of declarative knowledge than procedural knowledge. My own experience of working in Japan showed that this area was perceived by the majority of learners and teachers as the biggest area of need. This often results in learners lacking confidence in having the kinds of conversations they wish to have, particularly at lower levels of language proficiency. In this study, I wished to discover the extent to which explicit teaching of conversation strategies could offer learners a means of developing their conversational skills. This was observed via pre- and post-instruction interviews and learners' diaries, kept for a three-week period after instruction.

Results show an overall positive evaluation of the instruction from the learners. Pre-study interview data reveals that prior to instruction most learners tended to make use of only more general learning or communication strategies and not conversation strategies of the type taught. Diary data and post-study interviews indicate that learners felt they could make use of the strategies taught in conversations they had in a three-week period subsequent to the instruction and that they felt they helped with some common difficulties in conversation, including expressing ideas and feeling less anxious. They also reported that they perceived all conversation strategies to be useful but also that listenership and some means of taking account of others were easier to employ than others. Overall, results show that this approach is a plausible and useful means of developing conversation skills in this context.

133

The chapter begins with a review of some previous research in this area and the research questions used in this study. I then explain the methodology used in detail, before finally discussing the results of the study.

Previous research

As discussed in previous chapters, there have been a number of studies into the effects of instruction of general learning strategies (e.g., Gunning & Oxford, 2014), communication strategies (e.g., Dörnyei, 1995) and strategy use related to specific skills such as listening (e.g., Carrier, 2003). Studies of this nature have taken place in a number of EFL and ESL contexts with a variety of learners. There are also a number of studies which have employed action research designs (e.g., Nunan, 2002; Savaşçı, 2015). Results have often been positive, showing good effects in general for strategy instruction. Nunan (2002) for example, found that strategy training and reflection with university students in Hong Kong resulted in much more awareness and engagement in the process of language learning.

Several studies based on an action research model have been specifically targeted towards oral interaction. Kubo (2009) investigated the effects of asking students to record paired conversations outside class as a solution to learners' reluctance to speak in large classes. Participants were asked to record a twenty-three minute paired conversation regularly over an academic year and these were collected and analysed. Focusing on six pairs of lower-intermediate Japanese EFL students at university, Kubo analysed the effects via questionnaires, and measured the fluency of recordings (using speed as the main measure) over time. His findings show that participants reported increases in their confidence to speak for longer periods and that the fluency measures showed consistent increases over time. This demonstrates that a targeted intervention of this type can have clear effects and that action research can offer localised solutions to particular identified problems. As mentioned in chapter one, Talandis and Stout (2015) explored the effect of an intervention on 160 students taking compulsory English classes at a Japanese university from A1–B1 levels. The aim of this action research project was to address the difficulty many Japanese learners have in developing simple conversation skills in L2 English and included instruction on conversation strategies. The results (measured through three cycles of action research) used questionnaires, recorded paired speaking tasks and class notes. Results were very positive: showing a perceived benefit of the intervention from the majority of learners and an increased fluency and use of taught conversation strategies. This study demonstrates that a targeted approach can be used to develop conversation skills and that B1 level learners in particular appeared to benefit from the intervention. This current chapter focuses on a study in the same context, with students of B1 level, though it does not attempt such large-scale syllabus development and the focus is more tightly on four broad categories of conversation strategies identified in previous chapters. Nevertheless, Talandis and Stout's study demonstrates that positive results can be achieved with this type of intervention.

Savaşçı (2015) used action research to understand why learners in one EFL context (in this case Turkey), are reluctant to speak in class. Using questionnaires and semi-structured interviews, Savaşçı focused on twenty-two learners at a Turkish university. The findings show that the learners did not report language issues being a major factor in their reluctance to speak. Instead, chief reasons given were anxiety related to speaking, including fear of making mistakes and also the topic of the classes and whether it motivated them. One key reason for their language anxiety related to their fear of being judged by other Turkish learners and there was less perceived fear in talking to native speakers of English.

These results suggest that interventions such as Talandis and Stout's (2015) study in Japan, which in part focused on helping learners to have conversations about simple everyday topics, could be beneficial in many contexts. As mentioned in previous chapters, there is a tendency in many EFL materials to emphasise discussion of global topics of a slightly 'worthy' nature such as the problems with technology or the impact of tourism. While such topics can be of interest to learners (and few would advocate an exclusive diet of chatting about shopping and food), such topics can present a real challenge to L2 learners, who need to formulate their views as well as how to articulate them. This suggests that working on common everyday topics easily within a learner's ability can allow them to focus on how to say what they wish to say, something which may particularly benefit lower-level learners. These studies also show some of the potential of action research as a means of measuring the effects of interventions, in particular contexts. Interventions can be targeted at specific levels of learners, with specific needs, in specific settings. Smaller samples can be used as there is no comparison made to other groups and often the data uses at least one qualitative source. This allows us to investigate a particular problem in depth and find possible solutions which are (we hope) demonstrably effective. Teachers in other contexts may also find commonalities with their own learners and could then use a study as a model to conduct their own research.

The aim of this chapter is to offer one example of a study based on the model of action research outlined previously. It differs from some studies described above as I was not able to actually implement the results of the research, but it does seek to understand a possible solution to the problem identified previously - many Japanese learners have difficulty developing basic conversation skills in L2 English. In order to address this, as with chapter 4, instruction was focused on conversation strategies as described by McCarthy and McCarten (2018) and discussed in the previous chapters.

In undertaking this study, I sought to answer the following research questions:

RQ1. What are common conversational topics and reported difficulties?

RQ2. To what extent do participants themselves report use of taught conversation strategies in conversations outside of class?

RQ3. To what extent to participants perceive conversation strategies as useful tools to develop more successful conversations outside of class?

Methodology

As mentioned in the chapter introduction, a qualitative design based on an action research model was employed. The research had four stages: pre-instruction interviews, instruction, learning diary completion and post-study interviews.

Semi-structured interviews took place prior to the study in order to collect some basic biographical data and to understand which (if any) conversation strategies the participants were using or aware of prior to instruction the difficulties they had in conversations and topics they talked about. These were semi-structured in nature, meaning the interviewer uses the guide as a basis for framing the questions used but is also free to add follow up questions when the answer seems likely to reveal further interesting data (Dörnyei, 2007). Following this, participants were given four hours of instruction (in four classes) on conversation strategies (see procedure for details of this and the interview prompts used). Once instruction was completed, learners were also asked to keep a diary for three weeks, with two entries made per week. As with the diaries in chapter 4, these were structured and participants were given a template to follow, asking them to describe conversations they had, difficulties they had, any strategies used and the extent to which they thought these may have helped them. They were required to complete two entries per week. The aim of the diaries was to try and understand, from the participants' viewpoint, the extent to which they could recall and use the strategies taught and the extent to which they felt this helped them to develop more successful conversations. Following the completion of the diaries, semi-structured interviews were held with each participant, to understand which (if any) conversations strategies they had used and the extent to which they perceived the instruction to be useful.

Participants

Participants consisted of 12 Japanese students, drawn from a university programme in Chiba, Japan. All participants were at CEFR B1 level, based on placement tests undertaken. As stated in chapter 4, broadly, a learner at this level, is said to have the following competences:

> Can understand the main points of clear standard input on familiar matters regularly encountered in work, school, leisure, etc. Can deal with most situations likely to arise whilst travelling in an area where the language is spoken. Can produce simple connected text on topics which are familiar or of personal interest. Can describe experiences and events, dreams, hopes & ambitions and briefly give reasons and explanations for opinions and plans.

(Council of Europe, 2020, Table 1)

In terms of the specific conversational ability, a learner has the following competences:

> Can enter unprepared into conversations on familiar topics. Can follow clearly articulated speech directed at him/her in everyday conversation, though will sometimes have to ask for repetition of particular words and phrases. Can maintain a conversation or discussion but may sometimes be difficult to follow when trying to say exactly what he/she would like to. Can express and respond to feelings such as surprise, happiness, sadness, interest and indifference.

(Council of Europe, 2018, p. 85)

As acknowledged in the previous chapter, naturally, any learner who tests as being at this level may have these competences to a greater or lesser degree and will not have mastered them all.

Participants were all language majors, with a variety of second languages as their main focus of study: English (8), Spanish (2), Vietnamese (1), Chinese (1). Students with languages other than English as their major also took English classes as part of their studies. Eleven participants were female and one male. The mean age of participants was 18.1 and the ages ranged from 18-19. The mean length of prior English study was 7.5 years, ranging from 6 to 11 years.

The sample used here was purposive in that respondents had to be CEFR B1 level (as decided by placement tests) but as with the participants in chapter 4, the exact makeup of the sample was also partly due to convenience (which learners were available and willing to volunteer at the time of the study). This meant, for example, that it was not possible to get an even division of genders. All participants were living and studying in Japan at the time of the study and thus had opportunities to interact in English during their university classes, with some having English speaking friends outside of class. The nature of these participants (second language majors) meant they were, of course, a somewhat ideal sample as they were interested in language learning and thus highly motivated. I would not seek to claim that they represent completely typical young adult university level adult EFL learners in Japan, but they did share some core characteristics, such as having studied English as a compulsory foreign language for at least six years at school.

Procedure

All participants were given an initial semi-structured interview prior to instruction. The aim of the interview was to obtain basic biodata (such as number of years studying) and also to understand the extent to which participants were already using or had an awareness of conversation strategies, the difficulties they reported having in conversations and the topics they often talked about. A semi-structured design was chosen to allow follow ups for informative answers. The questions were based on design suggestions from Richards (2003) with initial biodata questions intended to relax and warm up the participants, before using a pattern of closed question /open question/ follow ups. This was to make it easy for participants to respond to respond initially (Richards 2003, p. 71), before the w/h questions and any follow ups allowed me to elicit as much as possible from each participant. The following prompts were used for pre-instruction interviews.

Warm-up (Biodata):

Can you tell me your name/age/how long you have been studying English?
Warm up:
Do you enjoy speaking in English?
What do you enjoy most /least about it?
Did you have any conversations in English in the last two weeks?
What was easiest /most difficult about them?
Can you think of a recent conversation which was difficult?
What was difficult about it?
Do you ever use strategies to overcome difficulties or help in conversations?
Which ones do/did you use?
Do you think they help?
Why/why not?

The post-study prompts were adapted from these and for obvious reasons, did not include the biodata questions. The final prompt was also added to understand whether any particular strategies seemed more difficult to use.

Post-study interview prompts

Warm up:
Thanks for the diaries. It's now three weeks since we had the classes. Have you got any general comments on what you studied or on keeping the diaries?
Now, I am going to ask some similar questions to the first interview.
Can you think of a recent conversation which was difficult or easy?
What was difficult/easy about it?
Did you use strategies to help you?
Which ones do/did you use?
Do you think they helped?
Why/why not?
Do you find any strategies difficult/easy to use?
Which ones and why?

Following the pre-instruction interviews, the participants were given four hours of instruction in four separate one-hour lessons, taught by the researcher. Due to COVID-19 restrictions, all classes took place online. Teaching was arranged to cover and recycle the four main categories of conversation strategies mentioned in chapter 4 and based on McCarthy and McCarten (2018, p. 12): showing listenership, managing the conversation as a whole, managing your own turn and taking account of others. Examples of the kind of language taught for each broad strategy and samples of how these were broken down can be seen in Table 5.1 (see appendix 5A for a description of everything taught).

Table 5.1

Samples of Conversation Strategy Instruction

Strategy/lesson	Sub-strategy	Sample language taught to realise the strategy
Showing listenership	Showing you are listening and interested	*Yeah, I can imagine/Uh-huh*
Managing the conversation as a whole	Showing you want to finish a topic	*So yeah, that's what I think*
Managing your own turn	Re-formulating	*I mean*
Taking account of others	Using vague language to describe likes/dislikes	*And that kind of thing/stuff, it depends*

Each strategy was covered equally and recycled across each class. Topics chosen to practise or contextualise the strategy were deliberately simple, to enable learners to focus on what they wished to say rather than what they might or might not know about a topic. The intention was also that each strategy could be used in any conversation learners may wish to have and was not linked to only one topic. As with chapter 4, the language used to exemplify each strategy was informed by the kind of spoken corpus research described in chapters 1 and 2. Jones et al. (2018), for example, show that 'So yeah + that's + brief summary' (e.g., *So yeah, that's what I think about X*) is one the most frequent chunks used by successful learners to show they wish to finish what they are saying.

As with the study in chapter 4, lessons were explicit in the sense that learners were told which strategies they were being taught the aim of each class was made clear to them. Each strategy was described in simple functional terms to learners e.g., showing you are interested when listening. Lessons were taught using a broad communicative methodology, with teacher-produced and authentic material used. Classes drew on principles common to communicative language teaching in general. As with the classes in chapter 4, these can be summarised as follows:

1. Language was explored in context.
2. Learners were guided towards understanding meaning and form by inductive means, such as teacher questions and exercises. This aims to foster noticing habits amongst learners. As mentioned in chapter 3, this belief, after Schmidt (1990, 2010), is that conscious registration of form(s) within the input can help learners to convert form(s) into intake when they encounter them and this increases the possibility that they will be able to use such forms, should they choose to.
3. Practice of the language was given in various forms - both in meaningful activities and in more controlled ways.

This did not mean all classes were organised in the same way – rather, the classes used the Illustration-Interaction-Induction (III) principles of McCarthy and McCarten (2018), as with chapter 4. These were employed flexibly and not as rigid lesson steps or stages.

The following sample of a lesson procedure gives an illustration of how these principles were employed.

Extract 1. Sample lesson procedure.

1. Warmer - think of a special event or festival you have been to. (There are a large number of festivals in Japan.)
2. Show a picture of a UK fireworks festival.
3. Ask students to formulate questions they wish to ask about the festival.
4. Re-formulate, then ask /answer these questions.
5. Teacher answers, including some vague language used in the class e.g., 'Is it dangerous?' 'It depends.'
6. Repeat some of the answers and ask students to note down the language used e.g., *'it depends'* / *'and things like that.'*
7. Discuss why we need to use vague language in this way. Check students understand that its use is partly to take account of the listener (we do not always need to include every detail in an answer).
8. Practice#1. Students repeat the vague phrases in context, focusing on good pronunciation and building up speed.

9. Practice#2. Students are asked to discuss and identify what vague expressions mean in context e.g., 'What are you doing for *Obon*? Going home. I want to see my family and everything.'
10. Practice#3. Students ask and answer simple questions e.g., 'What kind of music do you like?' using vague expressions as needed.
11. Practice#4. Describe a special event or festival you have been to. Your partner can ask anything they wish to. Don't say the name of the festival – they must try to guess. Use vague language as you need to.
12. Demo the same task with a student and this time you show listenership to show a) you are following, b) interested and c) empathetic. Students listen and note how the language you use is different to theirs. They should notice the listenership.
13. Get feedback and re-check why this is important.

Diaries

Participants were asked to keep a simple learning diary for a total of three weeks after the instruction, twice a week. This diary took the form of a template and learners submitted this online, once a week. The prompts used were adapted from the study in chapter 4:

Diary

Please write in this diary six times. 2 x per week, for 3 weeks. Use the format below (there are six of these below).

The English conversations you write about can be with friends, tutors, classmates or anybody else. They can be short or long, it does not matter.

Diary entry 1. Type as much as you like in each section but please avoid very short or one-word answers.

Name:

Date:

Describe a conversation (online or face to face) that you have had in English (who with?/where?/ what about?/how long?/how did you feel?).

Describe any difficulties you had in communicating.
Did you use any conversation strategies?

(If the answer is yes) Which strategy/ies did you use?

Describe how using the strategy affected your ability to have a successful conversation.

These prompts were designed to help the students to write each diary entry easily (given they were full-time students writing in L2 English) and also to encourage reflection and noticing of their use (or non-use) of conversation strategies. As mentioned in chapter 4, when we solicit diaries such as this from learners, there is a possibility that they may not truly reflect on how they felt but attempt to write what they think the researcher wants, knowing these would be read. It is also possible that they do not remember conversations they had easily. Although this is a weakness of this form of data collection, it is hard to imagine other ways we could collect such introspective data and there are many notable studies which have tracked different aspects of language learning (e.g., Pearson Casanave, 2013; Schmidt & Frota, 1986). The diaries were collected at the end of each week intervals to ensure learners were participating and completing them. A sample of one entry is given in Appendix 5B.

Data analysis

NVivo software (QSR, 2020) was used to sort and code the interview and diary data. As discussed in chapter 4, Computer-Assisted Qualitative Data Analysis Software (CAQDAS) software was chosen as it offers a greater level of objectivity than manual coding. CAQDAS software allows us to approach coding in a way which is more systematic and thus more objective than manual coding, creating categories and moving around the data with ease. These codes can then be checked using such tools as word frequency to ensure they accurately represent the views expressed in the data. This frequency data supports the ways in which we might categorise the data, adding a systematic and objective dimension to the analysis.

As the diaries all followed a template, answers were more restricted than the open-ended questions used to survey teachers in chapter 3. For this reason, the themes I chose to focus on were related to the template. These were:

Kinds of conversations students had

Difficulties encountered

Strategies used

The extent to which they were perceived to help

Interviews were coded in a similar way, with some ad hoc (in-vivo) coding when comments seemed to add to the data.

Results and discussion

In order to discuss the results, each research question will be considered in turn. The language of student responses has not been corrected.

RQ1. What are common conversational topics and reported difficulties?

Prior to the study, interviews showed that the kinds of conversations these participants had were most often with classmates and teachers, suggesting that this was the main site for practice. Topics of these conversations were generally in tune with the CEFR B1 descriptor which suggests learners at this level 'Can produce simple connected text on topics which are familiar or of personal interest.' (Council of Europe, 2020, Table 1). In the pre-study interviews these included: chatting, discussing social problems and volunteering, talking about likes and talking about music. These tallied with the diary data, where many similar topics were reported, examples of these were as follows:

- *We talked about what makes us happy and so on.*
- *I had conversations with my classmates on online. It was speed chat in Freshman literary class. We talked about where did we go as our school*

trip.

- *I talked with my friends on Zoom in my room. We talked about our favourite musicians about 15 minutes.*
- *I had d a conversation with my classmates on online. Today I had a English class and I talked about weekend plans and discussed some questions about country by my English teacher.*
- *I talked with my friends on Zoom about natto, because I do not like it.*

Set topics as part of classes were notably more 'discussion' orientated and more typical of discursive essays and exam tasks:

- *I had a discussion with my friends on online for 30 minutes. We talked about three topics, should kindergarten have English classes?, should we learn second language?, and why should we do homework?*
- *It was face to face, and today's topic was 'Describe a person who has a job that you admire.'*
- *I did a conversation with my 2 classmates in speaking English class about if rich countries like Japan or the US provide enough support to poor countries or not.*

In the interview and diary data, reported issues related to the following areas: problems with language, particularly vocabulary, problems relating to some form of anxiety about speaking and problems related to expressing or formulating ideas. Typical comments which reflected this were as follows:

Language issues

- *So, I have to know many vocabularies and idioms.*
- *Sometimes I didn't get other people to understand what I said. So, I have to know many vocabularies and idioms more than grammars.*
- *While speaking, I couldn't make much of grammar because I was panicked a little bit.*
- *It was difficult for me to express my exact feeling because of my less vocabulary and grammar skill.*
- *I forgot words I wanted to use while talking even if these words are simple.*

146

- *It was difficult for me to talk good expressions.*
- *I don't know a lot of word.*

Anxiety issues

- *After saying my opinion and listening opinion teacher said, there were silence. I tried to continue talking. And got panicked little bit.*
- *While talking, I wanted to add more details like giving examples to my idea to strength my opinion, but after I begun to talk for a while, I became to think I shouldn't talk more not to make mistakes.*
- *When I feel nervous, my mind go blank.*
- *I'm sometimes choked up and couldn't express what I was thinking.*
- *When I speak English, it's so nervous.*

Difficulty expressing or formulating ideas

- *I didn't have much knowledge about social problems.*
- *I couldn't express what I was thinking at all.*
- *I think that it was difficult to describe word. I wanted to talk about a night market but couldn't come up with a "market."*
- *It was kind of difficult to explain Japanese thing or Japanese word in English. I tried to use the easy words and explain clearly.*
- *I sometimes had a difficulties with express my thoughts clearly.*
- *The conversation topic was simple, but it was difficult to express my opinion in English.*
- *I chose "Arashiyama" in Kyoto as my favorite place, so it was difficult to express something unique to Japan in English.*

These comments reflect, to a degree, what we might predict. Conversations are of course more difficult if learners lack the language to express what they wish to say and the importance of vocabulary in second language learning is well-established. McCarthy (2004) and others have long argued that learning a core vocabulary based on the most common two thousand words in English is a vital target for learners. There is no reason to think this should not apply to conversations learners wish to have. These difficulties may also link to what participants report in relation to expressing their ideas. However, some comments in this area also seem to link to the topics learners were asked to discuss, particularly when they were more abstract or discursive. This may simply be because learners have not considered these areas in their first language or talked about them, so it is to be expected that they will be more challenging in an L2. One solution to this may be to give students topics which are within their comfort zone (McCarthy & McCarten, 2018) to allow them to focus on what they wish to say and managing their turn and the conversation. This was attempted in the instruction given within this study. Another is to simply give learners planning time for more challenging topics, something which has been shown to have positive effects upon fluency (Thompson, 2016). Regarding the types of anxiety which participants report, there is no simple solution to this, and it is well-established that affective factors are a significant variable which impacts upon language acquisition (Arnold, 1999). One solution may be simply to provide a supportive classroom and to keep re-iterating that mistakes are part of the process of learning to speak in a second language. Clearly, in this chapter (and book as a whole), I would also suggest that these kinds of difficulties may also be at least alleviated by teaching students conversation strategies and the language to realise them. As mentioned in the methodology section, the aim here was to introduce and practise strategies which could be used in any conversation students wished to have but to practise them by use of simple everyday topics.

RQ2. To what extent do participants themselves report use of taught conversation strategies in conversations outside of class?

RQ3. To what extent to participants perceive conversation strategies as useful tools to develop more successful conversations outside of class?

Pre-study interviews show very little awareness or use of conversation strategies. Those that were mentioned tended to be more general learning or communication strategies. Examples of these comments are as follows:

- *I use my vocabulary textbook.*
- *I'm trying to consult a dictionary if I have a problem.*
- *I try to remember some sentence such as 'could you explain?'*

The diary data and post-study interviews do show that participants report using the conversation strategies taught in conversations during the three weeks following instruction. Overall, although the data shows that all strategies were used, the most commonly reported two were taking account of others by using vague language, followed by showing listenership. Some examples of participants' comments from the diaries and interviews are as follows:

- *I used "so yeah" of strategy of managing the conservation when I want to show finish my topic.*
- *I used the conversation strategy that showing you're listening and interested.*
- *For example, when I talk why I think Kyoto is best place for foreign tourists who have never been to Japan, I said like that "I think Kyoto is best place because there are many traditional buildings. For example, Kinkaku temple, Kiyomizu temple, Inari shrines and things like that." And when others was talking I tried to say "That's nice", "That's amazing" and "I can imagine."*
- *I used "well", "That's ...", "Really?", and "So". For example, when we have to start talking, I said "So, we will talk about how we spent weekend. First..."*
- *And I want to tell many things to my classmates. So I use conversation strategy "something like that."*
- *When my classmates was speaking, I was able to say "uh huh."*
- *I used the phrase "So~"*
- *I used "Uh-huh" many times because I often listened to some classmates's opinions and stories. However, I could use the expressions "Yeah, I can imagine" and "I see" naturally.*
- *I use two phrases "and things like that" which I used describing why I decided studying Malaysia and "I'm not sure" which I used describing my opinion of building.*

149

- *I used 'uh huh', 'right', 'really?'*

A simple frequency search of this category using the NVivo software shows '*like*' as the most common word, with '*yeah*' the third, 'things' the fourth most frequent word with '*imagine*' the fifth most frequent. A search of these items shows that '*like*' and '*things*' were most often used to describe the use of 'and things like that' or 'and stuff like that' which was taught as part of the strategy taking account of others. '*Imagine*' and '*yeah*' were most often discussed in relation to '*Yeah, I can imagine,*' as part of the strategy of showing listenership.

It is pleasing that the participants could report and recall a range of strategies taught and the language used to realise them. It could be suggested that giving a slightly vague reply in order to take account of the listener may have been popular with these learners due to some of the difficulties related above, or be related to cultural norms of indirectness. If students feel pressured about thinking of an answer, they may believe it is also necessary to answer 'yes' or 'no' and an answer such as 'it depends' gives them the chance to show they are unsure. Similarly, phrases such as '*and things like that*' may remove the pressure to express every single detail of an answer and remember the vocabulary for that answer.

Participants also reported that, in general, they found the strategies to be useful. A search of word frequencies in NVivo shows that this is the sixth most common word in this category. There were several common reasons for this, many related to the difficulties reported previously: reduction of anxiety, ability to express ideas and the ability to speak more naturally. Typical comments are as follows:

Reduction of anxiety

- *I can express my feelings easily by using strategy. And it makes me fun during talking in English.*
- *By telling them that I was thinking, I was able to calmly organize what I wanted to say. By doing so, I was able to relax and enjoy speaking English a bit more.*
- *I think that using the strategy makes me confidence because I know correct words.*

150

- *"Really?" and "I can imagine" is reaction for speakers so It was good to make more comfortable atmosphere to talk and tell my thinking about the speaker's opinion.*

Expressing ideas

- *Making responses like uh huh or that's true brought me collaborative with others and by showing the end of my talking, it was easy for others to react to my opinion.*
- *When I couldn't say my opinion in detail, strategy avoid getting silence.*
- *I can express my feelings easily by using strategy. And it makes me fun during talking in English.*
- *While I was listening partner's opinion I said "That's good" "Really." I could show my feelings and listening. Also, my partner said same words when I was talking. I realized that these words make my feel relieved. Because I don't have to worry that whether my partner can understand or not.*

Speaking more naturally

- *I could have a natural conversation thanks to strategies showing I am listening and interested.*
- *I felt that my English is getting more natural compared to what I was using them (strategies) I'll keep be aware of using them.*
- *Using the strategy such as "uh huh" and "Yeah, I can imagine" makes the conversation more natural, and we can enjoy conversation more.*
- *Strategies make my speaking more natural.*

These results were confirmed by the post-study interviews, where participants repeated these ideas and explained the strategies used and if/why they found them to be useful. Typical comments are as follows:

- *It can avoid silence.*
- *Because if I couldn't use them, I couldn't talk my feelings well.*
- *If I don't answer anything to what someone says, the conversation stops.*
- *Sometimes when I am talking about my opinion there is silence. In such*

a situation I use strategy. I can avoid silence.

- *Strategy makes my conversation more smoothly and naturally. But for me, I have a lack of words.*

- *Especially, I used 'so yeah, that's what I think' helped me to show my talking and my classmates can talk easily.*

In the post-study interviews, participants were also asked which strategies they found easiest and most difficult to use. Listenership was the most commonly stated strategy which participants felt was easy, with nine of the twelve participants mentioning it. Others mentioned vague answers such as *'it depends'*, *'I'm not sure'* and *'and things like that.'* Common reasons given for listenership being easy to use were as follows:

- *It's easy to express my feelings.*
- *It can avoid silence.*
- *I have many opportunities to use these.*
- *It is like Japanese.*

These comments chime with the data from chapter 4. Listenership is likely to be easier because learners can focus on simply responding and do not have to formulate their own long turns. There are also direct similarities with Japanese and probably all languages, whereby it is common for listeners to show they are following and/or interested. The perception that vague answers were easy may relate to the difficulty and anxiety which these learners reported. As one said *I can use it (it depends) whenever I am not sure,* and this is likely to be when discussing more challenging topics such as those mentioned previously.

There was a great deal of variety in what participants found more difficult and there was no clear pattern to their answers. The focus here tended to be on certain expressions and not a whole strategy. Examples of typical comments were as follows:

- *'Yeah I can imagine.' I know the meaning but I have never used that expression.*
- *'I mean.' I want to be clear but don't know how to be clear.*

152

- *Long phrases 'so yeah that's what I think, pronunciation was very difficult.'*
- *'As I was saying' I don't know when I can use it.*

These comments seem to suggest that there were language issues with form in some expressions but also with function. The strategies and language taught operate within the discourse of conversations and so cannot be learnt just as an answer to a question. To use the example of '*I mean*,' this may be linguistically simple but to use it to reformulate, we have to know what we wish to reformulate and also how we wish to do so whereas when we show listenership, we simply have to listen and react.

Overall, the results are encouraging, as they show that learners could often recall strategies taught and report that they made use of them. Their perception was also that they were useful and that they seemed to help to lower anxiety, express their ideas and to speak more naturally. There was a good awareness that such strategies can help them to manage what they wish to say but also have a positive effect on the conversation as whole.

Unlike the data in chapter 4, the most commonly reported strategy was taking account of others (using vague expressions to do so), closely followed by showing listenership but participants did report using all strategies. This may have reflected the balance of the instruction given, as this was not weighted towards listenership in this case.

To return to the adapted action research cycle identified earlier, the problem identified was the low confidence and ability of Japanese EFL learners in relation to conversation skills. A qualitative study was planned and instruction given to address this by teaching conversation strategies and the language used to realise them. Results were then observed via participants' self-reports made in diaries and interviews. The problem identified was certainly evident in the reported difficulties which these participants had and there were a number of issues related to language (often vocabulary), anxiety and difficulty expressing or formulating ideas. What we can observe from the results is that instruction of conversation strategies, in this case at least, was perceived to help with these difficulties. Participants could remember the strategies taught and the language needed to fulfil them, they used a range of them and found they went at least some way to

153

addressing the difficulties reported. Although this is only one study, with one small group of learners, it suggests that teaching of conversation strategies may well offer a useful way forward for developing better conversation skills with Japanese EFL learners, particularly at this kind of level, where there is a simple base of language to work from.

My own reflection, having worked with these participants, is that learners in this context will be receptive to this type of instruction as it gives them some tools they can use in their own conversations. Using simple everyday topics within their comfort zones also helps to develop the ability to talk about such simple topics, a key competency at B1 level. This is discussed further in the concluding chapter of this book.

Conclusion

This chapter has described a qualitative study based on an action research model, using instruction in conversation strategies to address the difficulties many Japanese learners report having with conversation skills. The effects of the instruction were observed from learners' self-reports in diaries and interviews. Results show that these learners were not generally aware of these strategies prior to instruction and were able to make use of them in conversations in the three weeks following instruction. They were perceived to be useful as they enabled students to overcome some anxiety related to speaking, to express themselves more clearly and to speak more naturally. Overall, the results are positive because they show that instruction in this area offers a plausible solution for developing conversational skills with Japanese learners and chimes with the results of a larger study by Talandis and Stout (2015), which took place in a similar Japanese university context and also taught conversation strategies as part of its approach. Although the data was collected in Japan, there is also no reason why a similar experiment could not be used in other contexts where conversation skills cause difficulty for learners and materials adapted to fit local needs.

There are clear limitations to this study. The first is that the nature of a study modelled on action research focuses on only one group of learners. Further studies following this model would be needed to allow clearer reflection and to observe similar results. This could then result in action related to teaching schemes and curricula addressing speaking skills in Japan, particularly at university level. Secondly, as noted, these participants were particularly motivated (as language majors) and it would therefore be helpful if this model was replicated across larger groups, with non-language majors. As the study by Talandis and Stout (2015) shows, this kind of approach has been shown to improve outcomes with a larger sample and range of students in the Japanese university context. If a large-scale study of that nature is impossible, the smaller scale of the current study could certainly be replicated by teachers with their own classes, in universities or at senior and junior high schools, where most teaching of EFL begins. The results here and from Talandis and Stout (2015) show that this kind of focus seems to be particularly beneficial for lower-level students up to and around B1 level. The same type of study could be undertaken to address the same issue in other local contexts where conversation skills development is an issue.

Appendix 5A - Instruction

Strategy	Sub-strategy	Sample language taught to realise the strategy
Showing listenership	Showing you are following	*Right, Uh huh, I see*
	Showing you are interested and reacting/responding	*Wow! Really? That's good/nice/interesting/wonderful/terrible/bad/awful Yeah, I can imagine, Yeah, I think so too.*
Managing the conversation as a whole	Returning to the topic	*As I was saying*
	Starting a new topic or conversation	*So*
	Showing you have finished what you want to say	*So yeah + that's + brief summary*
Managing your own turn	Adding ideas	*I also…*
	Giving yourself time to think	*Well,*
	Reformulating and adding clarification	*I mean*
Taking account of others	Using vague language to describe common likes/dislikes and to respond to questions	(I like rock, pop) *and things like that.* (I like rock, pop) *and stuff like that.* (They run towards the crowd) *and everything. I'm not sure. I don't know. It depends.*

Appendix 5B

Diary sample

Describe a conversation (online or face to face) that you have had in English (who with? / where?/ what about?/ how long? / how did you feel?)

I had a conversation online because today I had English class. I talked with my 2 classmates about famous sites around the world and what place in Japanese is good for foreign tourists who have never been to Japan. We talked about 30 minutes but the time was too short for us. We really enjoyed talking. I felt it was so interesting because other classmates have different opinions and ideas.

Describe any difficulties you had in communicating

It was difficult for me to talk good expressions. Sometimes my expressions were difficult to understand for listeners because I couldn't speak in English with right grammar and words. It is my improvement pointes.

Did you use any conversation strategies?

Yes, I did. I tried to use conversation strategies. But I couldn't use it a lot and when others were talking, it was difficult for me to interrupt the conversation.

(If the answer is yes) Which strategy/ies did you use?

I used some conversation strategies. For example, when I talk why I think Kyoto is best place for foreign tourists who have never been to Japan, I said like that "I think Kyoto is best place because there are many traditional buildings. For example, Kinkaku temple, Kiyomizu temple, Inari shrines and things like that." And when others was talking I tried to say "That's nice," "That's amazing" and "I can imagine."

Describe how using the strategy affected your ability to have a successful conversation

When I used the sentence "and things like that", listeners could think that Kyoto has many temple and shrines. I think to be able to imagine the situation is important to have more good conversation. And listeners maybe agreed that there are many traditional buildings in Kyoto.

And when I used the sentence "That's ~" I could tell speakers that I listen and understand what you said. And I also tell my fillings for speakers. One boy who talked looked happy when I said "That's nice."

That is why I think that using strategy like that is very affective to have a successful conversation. If I use more conversation strategies when speakers are speaking in next times, they will talking more comfortable.

References

Arnold, J. (1999). *Affect in language learning.* Cambridge Language Teaching Library.

Borg, S. (2016). Action research: Not just about 'results.' *Research Notes,* 66, 3–5. https://www.cambridgeenglish.org/Images/368333-research-notes-66.pdf

Carrier, K. A. (2003) Improving high school English language learners' second language listening through strategy instruction. *Bilingual Research Journal, 27* (3), 283–408. https://doi.org/10.1080/15235882.2003.10162600

Council of Europe (2018). *Common European framework of reference for languages: learning, teaching, assessment companion volume with new descriptors.* https://rm.coe.int/cefr-companion-volume-with-new-descriptors-2018/1680787989

Council of Europe (2020) Global scale common reference levels. https://www.coe.int/en/web/common-european-framework-reference-languages/table-1-cefr-3.3-common-reference-levels-global-scale

Cutrone, P. (2009). Overcoming Japanese EFL learners' fear of speaking. *University of Reading Language Studies Working Papers,* 1, 55–63. http://www.reading.ac.uk/internal/appling/Cutrone.pdf

Dörnyei, Z. (1995). On the teachability of communication strategies. *TESOL Quarterly, 29,* 55–85. https://doi.org/10.2307/3587805

Dörnyei, Z. (2007). *Research methods in applied linguistics: Quantitative, qualitative and mixed methodologies.* Oxford University Press.

Edwards, E., & Burns, A. (2016). Language teacher action research: Achieving sustainability. *ELT Journal, 70*(1), 6–15. https://doi.org/10.1093/elt/ccv060

Gunning, P., & Oxford, R. (2014). Children's learning strategy use and the effects of strategy instruction on success in learning ESL in Canada. *System, 43*(1), 82–100. https://doi.org/10.1016/j.system.2013.12.012

Jones, C., Byrne, S., & Halenko, N. (2018). *Successful spoken English: Findings from learner corpora.* Routledge.

Koshy, E., Koshy, V., & Waterman, H. (2010). *Action research in healthcare.* Sage Publications.

Kubo, M. (2009). Extensive pair taping for college students in Japan: Action research in confidence and fluency building. *Accents Asia, 3*(1), 36–68. http://www.accentsasia.org/3-1/kubo.pdf

McCarthy, M. (2004). What constitutes a basic vocabulary for spoken communication? *JACET Summer Proceedings, 4*, 1–17.

McCarthy, M., & McCarten, J. (2018). Now you're talking! Practising conversation in second language learning. In C. Jones (Ed.), *Practice in second language learning* (pp. 7–29). Cambridge University Press.

MEXT (2014). *English education reform plan corresponding to globalization.* MEXT. https://www.mext.go.jp/en/news/topics/detail/__icsFiles/afieldfile/2014/01/23/1343591_1.pdf

Mori, Y. (2011). Shadowing with oral reading: Effects of combined training on the improvement of Japanese EFL learners' Prosody. *Language Education and Technology, 48*, 1–22. https://ci.nii.ac.jp/naid/110008686398/en/

Nunan, D. (2002). Learner strategy training in the classroom: An action research study. In J. C. Richards & W. Renandya (Eds.), *Methodology in language teaching: An anthology of current* practice (pp. 133–146). Cambridge University Press.

O'Sullivan, J. (1992). *Teaching English in Japan.* In Print Publishing.

Pearson Cassanave, C. (2012). Diary of a dabbler: Ecological influences on an EFL teacher's efforts to study Japanese informally. *TESOL Quarterly, 46*(4), 642–670. https://doi.org/10.1002/tesq.47

QSR International Pty Ltd. [Computer software]. (2020). *NVivo.* https://www.qsrinternational.com/nvivo-qualitative-data-analysis-software/home

Richards, K. (2003). *Qualitative research in TESOL.* Palgrave Macmillan.

Rust, F., & Clark, C. (2007). *How to do action research in your classroom. Lessons from the Teachers Network Leadership Institute.* Teachers Network. https://teachersnetwork.org/tnli/Action_Research_Booklet.pdf

Savaşçı, M. (2014). Why are some students reluctant to use L2 in EFL speaking classes? An action research at tertiary level. *Procedia - Social and Behavioural Sciences, 116*, 2682–2686. https://doi.org/10.1016/j.sbspro.2014.01.635

Schmidt, R. W., & Frota, S. (1986). Developing basic conversational ability in a second language. A case study of an adult learner of Portugese. In R. Day (Ed.), *Talking to learn: Conversation in second language acquisition* (pp. 237–326). Newbury House.

Talandis, G., & Stout, M. (2015). Getting EFL students to speak: An action research approach *ELT Journal, 69*(1), 11–25. https://doi.org/10.1093/elt/ccu037

Thompson, C. (2016). Using guided planning and task sequencing to improve grammar instruction. *Seinan Gakuin University Center for Language Education Journal, 6,* 1–20. http://repository.seinan-gu.ac.jp/bitstream/handle/123456789/1681/le-n6v1-p1-15-tho.pdf

Conclusion

Introduction

The intention in this final chapter is to draw the findings of this book together and suggest what the implications might be in terms of both teaching and possible future research. In doing so, it is worth repeating the caveat in my introduction: I have not been attempting to suggest that this is *the* way of helping learners to develop conversation skills. Rather, I have been trying to provide evidence that this may be *a* plausible way to help students in this area. Many teachers will have experience of learners complaining that despite all their efforts, they still find having a conversation in English a real challenge, at whichever level of proficiency they are at. This book has therefore been an investigation into how we might tackle this problem. There are also implications for how we could research this and related areas in the future. Although I have tackled this from several angles, there are other research designs which could be used in future and as with any research, it is clear there are limitations to the designs and data in this book.

This chapter begins by giving four implications for teaching and then four for research before I briefly list some limitations of this book and then offer a final word.

Four implications for teaching

1. Chapter 2 shows clearly that both native speakers, ELF users and successful learners do use conversation strategies to manage their own contributions and their interaction within conversations. It therefore seems logical to use this information to inform how we help less able learners to develop their conversation skills. As mentioned, it may be the case that learners develop these skills over time via interaction but as with pragmatic competence, this may be many years in coming (Halenko & Jones, 2017). This is time which learners may not have and it is also the case that many take classes to speed up this process. Focussing on how people actually have conversations allows us to get quickly to a way of helping them in this area and I would suggest that in a classroom, it is likely

to be of more value than the type of speaking practice which is often featured in communicative materials. Speaking in this sense is often a means of practising a (written) language feature and can all too often be far removed from the messier interaction of conversations. Focusing on conversation strategies can give us a way to organise teaching in this area, allowing for illustration of common linguistic realisation of strategies and practising them in context. The materials in chapters 3, 4 and 5 illustrate this.

Chapter 1 and the introduction also suggest that it is useful for teachers to view conversations quite differently to written language. They contain their own discourse and linguistic features and materials, exercises and practice need to reflect this. Why teach grammatical forms such as non-defining relative clauses in conversation in the same way as they appear in writing when we know they are often used by speakers across turns to comment on what they or others have said? In the preamble, I mentioned that one failure of my early teaching was that I did not recognise the sometimes quite different nature of spoken language. This meant I wasted time on activities such as asking learners to tell stories and then judging their output based on what we might expect from a written story. In the current age, there is no need to do this. We have a mass of evidence from spoken corpora about how conversations work, and it seems perverse not to use this.

2. The second implication is that the evidence in this book shows that focussing on conversation strategies can work to increase learner awareness and use of such strategies. Teacher evaluation of materials also showed that they found this a plausible approach. This suggests that as a means of designing materials and courses it is something worth trying, particularly in contexts where having conversations is a particular difficulty. To do so, teachers could work with published materials in this area (e.g., McCarthy et al., 2014). The principles of illustration, interaction and induction (McCarthy & McCarten, 2018, also see chapters 3, 4 and 5 of this book) can also be followed to make localised materials and procedures, if resources allow. This could mean adapting corpus data (see chapter 2 for one sample open access ELF

163

corpus) or using interesting literary/TV dialogues to illustrate particular strategies in context (e.g., Jones & Oakey, 2019). Further activities can then be designed to help with the principles of interaction and induction within a broad communicative framework. As mentioned, chapters 3, 5 and 5 give some examples of this type of material and these can easily be adapted. Obviously, any type of material needs to be sensitive to the local context, level of students, time allowed and so on.

3. The third implication is that communicative competence could act as a guiding principle when developing classes in this area. As mentioned in the introduction, communicative approaches have many benefits but there is still a tendency to focus on linguistic competence above all else. This risks foregrounding knowledge of form above knowledge of function, when Hymes' (1972) formulation of communicative competence makes clear that one cannot be separated from the other. Teaching conversation strategies is one example which shows that linguistic, pragmatic, discourse and strategic competences are interconnected. Learners cannot really hope to have a successful conversation without knowing how to say something, whether it is appropriate, how it works within and across turns and how we can use it to oil the wheels of a conversation. It may seem curious to rely on a theory formulated some fifty years ago but it is one that I have tried to demonstrate can be very effective in informing teaching.

4. The final implication is for teachers to focus classes on simple, everyday topics which align with CEFR level descriptors, particularly as they apply to conversations. As mentioned in chapter 4, one suggestion is that at B1 level, learners "Can enter unprepared into conversations on familiar topics" (Council of Europe, 2018, p. 85).

Using such topics can allow students to focus on how to say what they want and not on their own knowledge of topics or on searching for ways to formulate their ideas. Levelt (1989) importantly described the aspects of speech production as consisting of conceptualization, formulation and articulation. The constant use of slightly worthy topics in discussion classes can cause learners to stumble at the first

164

hurdle of conceptualization. This is not, of course, to say that topics of conversations should be childishly simple or focused only on such textbook staples as holidays or avoid anything more 'weighty.' There is obviously value in talking about such things, particularly if students wish to do so. I am really suggesting that simple, everyday topics need to be exploited more to reflect the common things people actually talk about. For example, talking about food might entail sub topics such as explaining what you like and don't like, describing food from your own country when studying overseas, talking about processes as you cook something with a housemate or deciding on somewhere to eat together.

Four implications for research

1. I hope that this book has shown that it can be useful to investigate an area from several angles, using different research designs. This helps to triangulate results and to employ quantitative and qualitative data to answer research questions. This seems especially useful in classroom-based research, where there a number of variables at play. Using mixed-methods and different designs may help us to "achieve a fuller understanding of a target phenomenon" (Dörnyei, 2007, p. 164). This could be applied in the future to this or other approaches which seek to foreground and develop conversation skills such as Meddings and Thornbury's (2009) ideas relating to conversation-driven teaching.
2. While the data in this book show the efficacy of teaching conversation strategies with the studies I have undertaken, there is clearly a need to investigate this more widely. One obvious area is of course to apply the same designs used in other EFL and ESL contexts. Another is to understand how conversation strategies might develop the communicative competence of either low- or high-level learners, two groups who only occasionally appear in studies of this type. We might also undertake similar types of materials evaluation using *while* and *post-use* evaluation as well as *pre-use* evaluation.
3. In much of the instructed SLA literature, there is often a lack of studies which investigate what learners actually do as a result

of instruction, when communicating outside of the classroom. This includes how they have understood it and how they use it, if they use it at all. The diary studies in chapters 4 and 5 are an attempt to understand what actually happens when we teach learners conversation strategies. Discussing the distinction between input and intake, Badger (2018) makes this point when he argues that the use of diaries as a form of autoethnography is useful because it enables us to track an individual's learning and how/if they are noticing language as they encounter and use it. A number of studies with individual learners across several contexts could be developed as case studies and these would provide a body of interesting evidence regarding what happens after instruction. We might ask, for example, as in chapter 5, what conversations learners had outside the classroom, what difficulties they had and if/how they used conversation strategies in those conversations. If learners are able to write in their L1, we could also allow more extensive diary entries, where they could comment on other aspects which influence communicative competence, such as affective factors. There is also no reason why diaries could not be produced in audio format and then transcribed by researchers. There are always questions about the reliability of such data (learners may not remember which conversations they have had, for example), but as mentioned in chapter 3, such criticism can be levelled at most types of qualitative data.

4. As chapter 1 and the rest of this book have attempted to show, the importance of using corpus data to inform how we understand conversations is clear. In chapter 1, I attempted to show the usefulness of understanding what non-native speakers say as they navigate conversations and which strategies they use. The rest of this book has shown how we can apply this kind of information to teaching and course materials. Future studies could investigate this by, for example, contrasting the effects of corpus-informed materials in this area with standard materials. Corpus studies investigating the features of conversations could also investigate in more depth what successful speakers do in conversations in both linguistic and non-linguistics terms. Aligning conversation strategy use with gesture, for example, would be interesting areas of future

research, and multi-modal corpora increasingly allow this (see Adolphs & Carter, 2013, for a discussion of these types of corpora).

Limitations

As with any research, there are clear limitations to this book, which I have tried to acknowledge in each chapter. The first is the fairly small sample size of the mixed-methods study in chapter 4. Ideally, studies of this nature should be undertaken with larger groups and although Dörnyei (2007) suggests fifteen per group is probably the minimum for an experimental design, bigger numbers are of course desirable to improve the power and reliability of the results. The second is related to the same study in chapter 4. In this chapter it was explained that a delayed test was not possible due to the absence of students caused by COVID-19 restrictions. Such tests need to be added as they offer evidence of durable learning (Schmitt, 2010) and will ideally be after delay of at least two weeks. This does not invalidate the test results in this chapter but as noted, it means that we can only argue that instruction had a short-term effect. It also shows the common difficulty of obtaining a large enough sample over the course of a classroom research study, something rarely discussed in the literature (see Nunan, 2005 for a discussion of classroom research).

The next limitation relates to the sample in chapter 5. As noted, the participants were language majors and as such likely to be highly motivated and engaged. They were, in many ways, an ideal sample. Future studies in this and other contexts could be undertaken with participants from other contexts such as high school, where motivation levels and engagement will vary. It would be particularly interesting to use a similar action research approach in situations where there is a clear lack of motivation, a phenomenon in many compulsory classes round the world (Sakui & Cowie, 2011).

In chapter 3, I needed to rely on pre-use materials evaluation, for reasons noted in the chapter. While this type of materials evaluation has validity, future studies could also usefully include post-use evaluation. This is simply because the potential of a piece of materials is often changed via our experience of it in actual use. As the nature of such evaluation is qualitative, a large sample is not necessary, provided it contains teachers in a range of EFL and ESL contexts.

Finally, a book of this type is limited by what I could practically undertake in the time I had. Ideally, the studies in chapters 4 and 5, for example, would be replicated in other ESL and EFL contexts to offer comparisons and add breadth to what we can imply from the results. Replication studies are limited in the instructed SLA field (Schmitt, 2010) and future studies could certainly use the same designs in other contexts.

Final word

Having a successful conversation in a second language (whatever level of proficiency you are at) is one of the most rewarding aspects of learning a second language. You get immediate feedback, you connect with someone else, you express yourself and for a few minutes, you stop feeling like an infant in an adult's body, a frustration which will be familiar to many of us who have learnt another language. Conversation strategies are one plausible way in which instruction can facilitate this and I hope this book has provided some evidence which will encourage teachers to try the ideas out in their teaching.

References

Adolphs, S., & Carter, R. (2013). *Spoken corpus linguistics: From monomodal to multimodal.* Routledge.

Badger, R. (2018). From input to intake: Researching learner cognition. *TESOL Quarterly, 52*(4), 1073–1084. https://doi.org/10.1002/tesq.448

Council of Europe (2018). *Common European framework of reference for languages: Learning, teaching, assessment companion volume with new descriptors.* https://rm.coe.int/cefr-companion-volume-with-new-descriptors-2018/1680787989

Dörnyei, Z. (2007). *Research methods in applied linguistics: Quantitative, qualitative and mixed methodologies.* Oxford University Press.

Halenko, N., & Jones, C. (2017). Explicit instruction of spoken requests: An examination of pre-departure instruction and the study abroad environment. *System, 68*, 26–37. https://doi.org/10.1016/j.system.2017.06.011

Hymes, D. H. (1972). On communicative competence. In J. B. Pride & J. Holmes (Eds.), *Sociolinguistics* (pp. 269–293). Penguin.

Jones, C., & Oakey, D. (2019). Literary dialogues as models of conversation in English Language Teaching. *Journal of Second Language Teaching and Research, 7*(1), 107–135. https://pops.uclan.ac.uk/index.php/jsltr/article/view/583

McCarthy, M., & McCarten, J. (2018). Now you're talking! Practising conversation in second language learning. In C. Jones (Ed.), *Practice in second language learning* (pp. 7–29). Cambridge University Press.

McCarthy, M., McCarten, J., & Sandiford, H. (2014). *Touchstone second edition, levels 1-4.* Cambridge University Press.

Meddings, L., & Thornbury, S. (2009). *Teaching unplugged: Dogme in English language teaching.* Delta Publishing.

Nunan, D. (2005). Classroom research. In E. Hinkel (Ed.), *Handbook of research in second language teaching and learning* (pp. 225–240). Lawrence Erlbhaum Associates.

Sakui, K., & Cowie, N. (2011). The dark side of motivation: Teachers' perspectives on 'unmotivation.' *ELT Journal, 66*(2), 205–213. https://doi.org/10.1093/elt/ccr045

Schmitt, N. (2010). *Researching vocabulary: A vocabulary research manual.* Palgrave Macmillan.

Publication Information

Published by Candlin & Mynard ePublishing Limited, Unit 1002 Unicorn Trade Centre, 127-131 Des Voeux Road Central, Hong Kong.

For further information about Candlin & Mynard, please see the website: http://www.candlinandmynard.com

This edition was republished by Candlin & Mynard in ebook and print formats in 2021.

Positive Pedagogical Praxis Series

https://www.candlinandmynard.com/ppp.html

Edited by Tim Murphey

Titles in the series

Learner-Controlled Tasks for the Autonomy Classroom: A Teacher's Resource Book by Christian Ludwig and Lawrie Moore-Walter

Voicing Learning by Tim Murphey

Conversation Strategies and Communicative Competence by Christian Jones

The Personalized Learning Module: A Collection of Learning Advising Tools by Stephanie Lea Howard, Tarik Uzun, and Gamze Guven Yalcin

Printed in Great Britain
by Amazon